R.L. ADAMS

All Rights Reserved

Legal Notices

The Author was complete as possible in the creation of this book. in this publication, the Author assumes no responsibility for errors, omissions, or contrary interpretation of the subject matter herein. Any perceived slights of specific people or organizations are unintentional.

WEB

3.0

STARTUPS

ONLINE MARKETING STRATEGIES FOR
LAUNCHING & PROMOTING ANY
BUSINESS ON THE WEB

R.L. Adams

CONTENTS

INTRODUCTION

The Internet is evolving at an uncanny rate. Websites launch. Websites fizzle. News comes. News goes. Everything happens in the blink of an eye. That's the Internet – a virtual blur of information floating around in Cyberspace, throbbing and pulsating with data. To some, access to it is considered a standard of living, but to others it's simply still a marvel.

No matter how you look at it, the Web molds and shapes nearly every aspect of our lives today, from how we live, to how we interact, to how we work. And, no matter who you are or what you do, the Internet is playing a major role in your life right now, in some way, shape, or form. It is affecting you and every other living, breathing, human being on this earth, and shaping decisions both big and small.

Most of us have become experts in navigating this expansive Web. We can seek out and find what we're looking for relatively quickly all thanks to the ease of online search. It's almost second nature to us now. When we need to know something we hit the Internet, and we've all become self-proclaimed experts at it. We search with our laptops, our desktops, our mobile phones, and tablets.

We ask questions like: "How relevant is this?" or "Do my friends recommend this?" and "How do I get to this address?" It happens each and every second of the day, millions of times over. We are constantly seeking to understand, learn, and absorb answers to our questions from the vast bits and bytes of information stored online. But, where the disconnect lies is not in our ability to search for relevant information as consumers, it's in our inability to be found as business owners.

It is much more difficult, today, in the new era of the overcrowded Web, to be found as relevant. It's this relevancy that has become the desired target of so many marketers and business owners constantly vying to get in front of the consumers' eyes. But, it's also this same relevancy that is becoming increasingly difficult to achieve over time as the Web continues to expand and grow.

The one company that has single-handedly helped to manage our ever-expanding Web today, and push its vast contents closer and closer to relevancy, is Google. Google has poked, prodded, and razed the Web, making it more efficient and more relevant through the use of its own algorithms. It has fine-tuned in some areas, and has launched all out attacks in others. Because of this, many people feel lost, overwhelmed, and intimidated because they simply don't know how to get found.

The necessity to bring together so many different marketing disciplines can leave even the hardest working entrepreneurs at bay when trying to appear visible on the Web. Having to converge relevancy across so many different channels from organic search to social media can be incredibly difficult, especially if you don't know what you're doing.

But, for the few that do understand the Web and its new rules, and can bring together marketing savvy across all of its many channels and disciplines, bountiful success awaits. These are the trusted few who have become the organic engineers of business success stories near and far. However, to truly succeed today, and truly make significant strides towards a successful startup on the Web, you must understand and harness the new rules of the Web, Google's new rules.

Today, success can only come to those who can leverage Google's new rules in an effort to dash towards the single most important concept of ranking a Website today, and that is relevancy.

In today's new Web – Web 3.0 – relevancy is the name of the game.

If you can't be found, you're not relevant, and if you're not relevant, you're lost in the sea of Cyberspace, floating around like a ship without a sail and eventually you become irrelevant.

THE WEB 3.0 STARTUP

In the Web 3.0 economy, you are only as good as you are relevant. If you can't be found in either organic searches on the Web or recommended through crowd-sourced social media channels, then no matter how great your products are, or how incredible your services may be, your business will falter and fail.

A Web 3.0 startup must address an individual's desire to seek out and find a business through a relevant search, while also being able to be located and recommended through social media and crowd sourced channels. A successful Web 3.0 startup brings together the cohesive nature of Google's new Internet search rules and the convergence of social networking mediums into one laser-targeted approach.

MARKETING IN A WEB 3.0 ECONOMY

For many, dealing with online marketing on its own can be complex to tackle. But, in the new Web 3.0 economy, it's become even more difficult. Today, whether it's social media strategies, blogging, securing business reviews, or understanding search engine optimization, many average business owners are left overwhelmed and frustrated.

Many can surf the Web, but when it comes time to implementing strategies for finding customers, they feel lost. And for most, the simple thought of having to figure out new ways to constantly market can consume and interrupt their entire lives. But it doesn't have to be that way.

Although the Web is large, and online marketing has become extremely diverse, most business owners simply have to learn and understand where to turn when it comes to marketing advice. With so many different resources available for different aspects of the Web's many marketing mediums, it's no wonder people get confused and feel lost. They get excited after reading about startups, but they don't know how to get that startup off the ground.

In my more than decade-long pursuit of everything marketing online and offline, I've come to learn what works and what doesn't for being able to connect with customers quickly and efficiently. *Web 3.0 Startups* is the culmination of my expertise in the field of marketing on the Internet, and more importantly, the art of getting found organically.

Look, we all want to be able to focus on our core businesses right? I'm sure that you would rather be honing your service or building a better product than having to try to find new ways to connect with potential customers. But you know, as well as I do, that no matter how good your product or service is, that without effective marketing, you're nowhere.

Marketing is important, that's clear, but also knowing how to market in the new Web 3.0 economy is critical to the success of your business. I have literally immersed myself in this subject and understand just what it takes to market almost any product or service from its conception through to its fruition, and this book is the culmination of that experience.

A NEW BREED OF MARKETERS

Just as fast as you were able to blink your eyes over the past few years, up emerged this new breed of marketing and marketers. This is Web 3.0 marketing. What is it? Well, back in 1999, the term Web 2.0 was coined to refer to technology on the Web that went beyond just static Webpages. The term has been used to widely represent the new era of Websites that have emerged onto the scene offering rich user experiences. But that was then, and this is now.

Today, we are living in the Web 3.0 economy. Web 3.0 is more than just dynamic Websites that are interactive; it's more than just rich user experiences. Web 3.0 is the synergy of the Web in ways never seen before. Web 3.0 is the interaction of Web with the mobile Web and our social interactions across all platforms.

Tackling the launch of a startup in the Web 3.0 economy involves a specific skillset of the capability to appear relevant and visible to consumers searching for your goods or services. You must be able to understand the new set of rules that have evolved, and how to adapt your marketing activities to them. Not only is it important to be able to connect with customers one-on-one today, but you also must be able to connect through social aggregation as well.

All of this can seem overwhelming, but in this practical guide, I will teach you just what it takes to launch and promote your business in the Web 3.0 economy from the ground up. We will take a look at some of the foundational principles of how to set yourself up for success, and extend into some specific marketing methods and techniques for getting up and running quickly and cost efficiently. Here are the marketing methods that we'll be analyzing:

1. **Organic marketing method** – The organic marketing method involves your ability to appear relevant in Google search results when consumers are searching for your products or services. The organic marketing method will involve some SEO strategy and implementation.

2. **Social marketing method** – Social media strategies that work will be the topic of discussion. I analyze and recommend what works and how it works, along with the steps needed to take to institute strategies that create raving fans and get you sales.

3. **Referral marketing method** – The referral marketing method is one of the most powerful drivers of business, but in the Web 3.0 economy, you can harness strategies that will get you receiving referral business faster and more frequently than ever before.

By creating a three-pronged approach to marketing in the Web 3.0 economy, you will be able to solidify your brand in your particular niche. While the marketing principles and techniques discussed in this book do not take rocket science to implement, they do take a concerted and committed effort on your part. Without this commitment and consistency in implementation, day-in, and day-out, you will see your marketing efforts fail.

In the pages of this book, I will reveal to you just how to take your business from literally ground zero, to generating a tremendous amount of leads and sales by implementing marketing methods that anyone can implement with little to no marketing budget.

WHO THIS BOOK IS FOR

This book is designed and written for virtually anyone who's looking to expand his or her knowledge of marketing a product or service on the Web. Whether you're a freelancer, a brick-and-mortar business, or a licensed professional in any field, understanding how to market yourself and your business in the Web 3.0 economy is paramount to your success.

Let's face it, most average people don't have the budget for a lofty marketing department for their business. And, in fact, most people simply venture out on their own onto the World Wide Web in the hopes of securing a future with a steady income. Most of these people simply don't have the time to try to deconstruct and analyze what works and what doesn't for marketing on the Internet.

Most people feel lost when it comes to marketing on the Internet. Not only is the face of the Internet evolving at such a rapid pace, the methods and mediums are shifting as well. Take for example the major changes instituted to Google's search engine algorithm over the past few years. Without understanding what happened and how you need to approach optimizing your site and your offer in the Web 3.0 economy, you'll be struggling to get by and be found relevant.

Marketing can be difficult, virtually anyone can tell you that. Most people are simply so busy working in their businesses that they find difficulty devoting the time to working on their businesses. And sometimes, it can feel like a steep uphill battle trying to get your message out onto the Web. With the rise and popularity of social media, the level of noise has increased so much that sometimes, even with access to 7 billion people at your fingertip, you're barely able to make a ripple in the ocean of commerce.

In this book, I will take a lot of the guesswork out of marketing in the Web 3.0 economy, and what you can to do begin making strides towards an efficient delivery of your message to your target consumer. When applied consistently over time, these methods and techniques will lead to the establishment of a solid brand foundation for you to implant your success in the marketplace. But this is not going to happen overnight.

In marketing, you either have to have a lot of money or a lot of time. When you have a lot of money, and you can spend millions on customer acquisition, as long as you have a solid product or service to back it up, you will succeed. However, we all know that most of the entrepreneurs and business professionals hitting the scene are not filthy rich. Most people just want to find practical ways that they can market and promote on little to no monetary investment.

If you fit this bill, and you're like most others who

don't have a small fortune to spend on marketing your new or existing business, then the practical methods, techniques, and principles of this book are for you. While these methods and techniques require little to money to institute, they do require consistent effort over an extended period of time. You must be able to place your commitment in the form of time to marketing your business the right way in the beginning. If you don't, you will quickly see yourself fail.

This is especially true when you first start out because you'll be taking the necessary steps to create a solid foundation for which to build your business platform from. By simply doing a little bit each day in each of the areas of marketing focus, you will be able to successfully tackle online marketing for your business in the Web 3.0 economy.

HOW TO READ THIS BOOK

I've read a lot of books on marketing. A lot. I didn't want this book to be filled with too much theory so although I will discuss some theory behind each of the steps to marketing and positioning your business online, I focus more on the practical methods of how to institute them. When you're reading this book, I would recommend that you read it straight through because it's important that you ensure that your foundation and your brand is in place before trying too hard to push your message out there.

However, I do understand that some people are picking up this book that have a mild background in online marketing, or already have a business up and running that they're looking to find more ways to help promote online. If that's the case for you, then feel free to skip ahead to the sections as you see fit. If you feel like you've already conquered any of the areas or topics discussed, then by all means, move forward from there.

I'm guessing, however, that if you're picking up this book, then you at least need some help in marketing yourself on the Web. Try not to overlook some of the important aspects of your business and your brand because that may be where you're faltering. Without a strong foundation and brand, pushing a message will feel like pushing against a 2-ton rock that hasn't moved in a century. It will be difficult.

While the methods and techniques discussed in this book are fairly straightforward, understanding some of the concepts and principles behind why and how they work in the Web 3.0 economy is part and parcel to your overall success. You can't institute something you don't understand, because while you may be able to have some success with it at first, you won't understand its overall meaning towards the complete marketing knowhow for continued and lasting success.

1
BUILDING A SOLID FOUNDATION

I know that you're bombarded with information every minute of the day. People jump and scream touting that they have the next big thing, or the biggest secret to succeeding online. It gets tiresome after a while doesn't it? Personally, to me, I've sifted through hundreds of books on the subject of marketing, and even more books on technical skills for design, copy writing, software design, and everything in between.

In the past, I've been able to find a gem here and there – that one book out of dozens that stands out and actually provides real usable information that can instantly make a measurable difference in the advancement of that skill. But we all know it doesn't happen often. What usually happens is that authors get so caught up in writing about theories, that they forget to actually provide real usable steps that need to be taken in order to successfully execute a marketing concept. That won't happen here.

Why should you listen to me? Well, I've spent the better part of my life immersed in the study of marketing and design. I'm versed in not only the theory of it all, but also in the technical and aesthetic aspects too. I understand how the Web works, how to build solid brand awareness, how to be found online, and how to deliver a strong marketing message that sells. I understand how to turn an idea or concept into marketing gold, and I know how to do it with virtually no money out-of-pocket.

In the last several books that I've released, I've addressed various different topics from SEO, to book marketing, and beyond. This book is going to be a fusion of a lot of similar concepts to building a solid brand foundation, then successfully positioning yourself in organic search, as well as through social mediums.

Look, a lot of different marketing mediums on the Web require inherent knowledge of technical skills that present themselves in fields like search engine optimization. To be found on Facebook, LinkedIn, and Twitter, you need to understand this type of information. In this book, I will convey all of my knowledge in that field, and in the field of marketing as well.

GETTING STARTED

There is so much to think about when you launch yourself as a businessperson or company on the Web that many people simply don't stop to address the marketing message that they're delivering in the process. It is very easy to get so caught up in the excitement of being able to promote yourself on the Web, that you don't take the time to analyze the core aspects of demographic targeting, brand building, and positioning, first.

You need to learn how to ask yourself intelligent questions about who you are, what you provide, and how you're better than your competition. You need to take the time to analyze the pros and cons of someone potentially doing business with you, and take a deep look at your offer to see if it's a viable one. You have to ask yourself questions like:

1.   Who is my target customer?

2.   What is my marketing message?

3.   Does my brand portray a professional image?

4.   Where do I find my customers?

5.   Who are my competitors?

6.   What are my competitive advantages?

7.   Does my Website attract, engage and convert?

8.   Am I leveraging social media the right way?

9.   Can people find me on Google searches?

Obviously, these are just some examples of the types of questions that you need to be asking yourself, but there is more, much more. And, although it can seem overwhelming at times, by breaking your marketing efforts up into several digestible components, then tackling a little bit each day, you will be on the path to business success in no time.

Where do we begin?

The first steps for any business, whether you are established or not is to know your customer. Do you know your customer yet? Who is he or she? How old is he or she? Do they live in a specific area? Where do they hangout? How can you get hold of them?

Once you understand your customer, you can begin to

build the foundation of your business from there. But for most people, they haven't taken the time to understand their customer, and without that understanding, there is no foundation for business success.

To start out, you need to determine your customer profile by looking at three different factors. Once you understand your exact target customer profile, it will be considerably easier to determine the best avenues for marketing to them online. Here are the factors involved:

1. Customer Demographic

    a. Age

    b. Gender

    c. Income level

    d. Occupation

    e. Education

    f. Family circumstance

        i. Married

        ii. Divorced

        iii. Single

        iv. Children

2. Lifestyle and Geographic Factors

    a. Where do they live?

    b. Where do they spend their time?

  c. Does weather play a role?

  d. What activities do they engage in?

  e. How do they spend their money

3. Customer Needs

  a. What does this customer need?

  b. When do they need it?

  c. Where do they usually go to find it?

  d. How large is the demand?

  e. What price are they willing to pay?

By answering questions like who your customer is, how old they are, where they live, where they spend their time, what do they need, and where do they usually get it, you will be able to stitch your precise target audience to market your products and services to. At first, answering these questions may seem like a waste of time. It's pretty obvious you know your target customer right? Well, regardless of whether or not you do, you have to identify them specifically in as much detail as possible.

For example, if you're targeting mothers between the ages of 30 and 45 years old, find out where they spend their time and where they live. If they live in a specific area, does weather affect their activities? If it rains a lot in that area, where do they normally go when it rains? How does the rain affect their activities? Do they spend a lot of time in the car because of this? Or, if the weather is nice, where do they usually go?

All of these questions and more can be used to stitch

together a customer profile for your ideal customer. The more you actually get to know your customer in the beginning, the more success you will have in your marketing efforts down the road.

Now, you may be thinking that your customer profile falls into a wide spectrum of people. This is the wrong frame of mind. Narrow it down. Pinpoint it exactly so that you have an exact customer profile of whom you will be marketing to. The better you know your customer, the more successful you will be at marketing to them.

This may sound like very rudimentary basics, but this is highly critical to your success in marketing your business online. This information will not only help you market in the Web 3.0 economy, but it will also help you determine every business decision that you make both on and off the Internet.

Creating and refining your customer profile is one of the foundations for the future success of your business, so don't pass this up by simply assuming you know everything about your customer. Take the time to do the research accurately, and to the best of your ability. Pull out a pad and pen or launch your laptop's notepad. Whatever you have to do, do it and begin brainstorming and determining who you are going to be marketing to.

Do not skip this step. Take the time right now to answer the questions about your specific customer profile related to their demographics, lifestyle, geographic factors, and needs. Don't pass this off to someone else to do because understanding your customer and his or her needs is a vital element of the marketing process.

2
BUILDING YOUR BRAND

"Billions and billions served." Can you guess which company has this slogan? Yes, of course, it's McDonald's. What sets McDonald's apart from the rest of the burger joints out there? Sure, it has some competitors that are doing well, but McDonald's is a brand that has become a household name because they deliver on their unique value proposition of providing good food, fast.

What's a unique value proposition? This is a company's promise of value to be delivered, along with a belief from that customer that the value will be experienced.

When you see a slogan that says "billions and billions served," this is a testament to the value that McDonald's has to offer and it's also proof of that value. If billions and billions were served, it is clear that there is value there and that customers are experiencing value because they keep coming back for more.

McDonald's pretty much set the stage for the fast food concept. They have a solid brand, and you know just what to expect from that brand. They're consistent. Just like McDonald's, you need to develop your own unique value proposition. Whether you're already in business, or you're thinking about it, this is vital to your success.

Once you've gauged and understood your target customer profile, you must be ready to make them aware of your brand's values. Here are the four components of identifying your brand's values for creating your own unique value proposition.

1. **What are your brand's benefits?** – Explain just what your brand can do for the consumer. Try to answer the question "What's in it for me?" from the customer's perspective.

2. **What sets your brand apart?** – What do you do that's better than what your competitors already do? What's going to set you apart from existing, more established brands?

3. **What about your brand makes it relevant?** – Relevancy is a key factor in your unique value proposition. How is your brand going to solve the customer's problems, or bring value to their lives?

4. **<u>Do you have proof in your value proposition?</u>**
   – Like with McDonald's slogan, there is proof of its value proposition to its customers right there. Do you have proof yet of your own unique value proposition? If not, it's important that you get it by getting real customer feedback to your products or services.

As you answer these questions, you will be able to create your own unique value proposition. This is more important today than ever because as the Web 3.0 economy expands and grows, getting more and more crowded, the more you generalize your services, the more difficult it is going to be for you to gain visibility and traction in the marketplace. The more specific you can be in your entire way of thinking and approach, the more success you will have in the long run.

Think for a moment about H&R Block. When you think of that company, what comes to your mind? Does fast, affordable, and reliable tax services sound about right? Yes, of course. Their slogan is "Never settle for less." From their point of you, you should never have to settle for inferior tax services, implying that their tax services are superior. Their unique value proposition is that they provide cheap, high quality tax return services that saves consumers' time, and the hassle of having under qualified accountants prepare their returns and make costly mistakes.

How is this backed up? It's pretty clear by the millions upon millions of people who continue to use the company's services that is has proof in its unique value proposition. It is also clear that H&R Block is a leader in the industry, as it has virtually become a household name. How did it pull that off? The company laser-targeted its

30

unique value proposition to their exact specific customer profile, that's how. It was very, very specific.

When you think about that company, you know that you're going to benefit from it by getting fast, affordable, and reliable tax service. But not only that, this is what makes this brand stand apart from the rest; it makes the brand rise above the noise, and make it very relevant.

Although H&R Block is an extreme example of a very large company that has spent years honing their marketing message, the company had the right building blocks from the beginning. It spent the time to analyze its customers, and figured out exactly who they were. Then geared all of its marketing, online and offline, towards that customer. From slogan to logo design, to its colors and overall marketing pitch – they are all inline with its customer profile.

When you market to your customer profile, you are identifying with a specific type of person. If that person is frugal, then you need to be targeting cost savings; if that person enjoys the finer things in life then your imagery and verbiage should be of a higher-end, more luxurious one. Everything has to fall inline with your customer profile to succeed in any economy, but most importantly, in the ever-crowding Web 3.0 economy.

BRAND REPRESENTATION

The visual representation of your brand is important. By portraying a professional image that's in line with your brand's values, you successfully complete the foundational footing for your company.

You may already have a business, or you may just be thinking about starting a business. But no matter where you're at in your business or professional career, you have to understand that the visual representation of your brand is another vital pillar in the foundation to your business's success.

You must be prepared to ask yourself important questions about your business and just how well you've portrayed its visual representation. Think about questions like:

- How important is a logo to you? Is it something you think matters only a little?

- What colors are you using in your logo? What do those colors signify?

- Have you done the research into color theory to make sure that your subconscious message of your logo is inline with your conscious value message?

- How about your company slogan? How much time did you put into that if you're already in business, or how much time do you plan to?

Some people simply don't realize the importance of their visual representation to people of their brand. And while image isn't everything, it certainly means a lot in the ever-crowding world of the Web 3.0 economy.

When a consumer is first exposed to your company and your brand, their brains cycle through various patterns of identification. Without their knowledge, the brain is zeroing in on whether or not they identify with your brand.

This is where your unique value proposition comes into play and how well of a job you did to target the visual and literal representations of your company with its inherent value propositions. Why is this important? This is probably one of the single biggest detractors of a consumer when a company doesn't have a professional image.

Think about book covers for a minute. While a stunning and professional book cover won't entirely sell you on a book, it will certainly have you keen on thinking about buying it. However, when you see a very amateur, poorly designed book cover, how much does that detract you from the book? For most people the answer is a lot.

A similar concept applies to brand images. Consumers will expect you to have a professional image, so it won't completely sell them on your company. But, it also won't detract them as much as if you don't have a professional brand image, or if you have a very poor one.

Keep in mind that your brand image is going to be seen everywhere and you need to keep this consistent so as not to confuse consumers. This is because the brand will be your single biggest identifier. When consumers see your brand, they will identify with it in very specific ways that will determine whether or not they create a pre-existing notion of benevolence and trust towards it, or not.

LOGO DESIGN

Your brand is your identity and your logo identifies your brand. If you have a business and you don't have a professional logo, then you are selling yourself short. After you've taken the steps to identify your exact customer profile, you've envisioned your brand identity, and created a unique value proposition, you then need to translate that into a vivid image and slogan reflective of the professional nature and target consumer of your products or services.

Easier said than done right?

Yes, of course, it's easier said than done. We all know that we need a professional logo, but many people simply don't know where to turn. Or, they think that getting a professional logo will cost an arm and a leg. Well, let me tell you something: it doesn't matter what you have to do to get a professional logo designed, you simply need to do it. This should be your number one aim and priority after you've completed your customer profile, brand identity, and value proposition.

The landscape for businesses in the Web 3.0 economy is so competitive that without a professional logo you are really shooting yourself in the foot. By starting off with the solid foundation of a professional logo and slogan, you will set yourself up for success. Although image isn't everything when it comes to your logo, it certainly means a lot. It indicates to the consumer just how much time, effort, and attention to detail this business must have given its appearance.

I'm sure that you yourself can relate to this. You've seen bad logos before in your life. How do you feel about those companies? How much trust can you put into a business that doesn't see the value in creating a professional appearance to its customers? Not a lot by most people's terms.

Do what you have to in order to source a professionally designed logo. You don't have to pay a small fortune for it, but do expect to spend a good bit on it. This is important because it is the basis for your brand's identity. The colors and visual elements that you select should reflect your unique value proposition in the best way possible. Here are the various options when it comes to logo design:

- **Crowd-sourced designers** – If budget is at issue, you may want to consider using a Website like 99designs.com. The site allows you to post your design project and receive designs from up to 99 designers. The project fee is kept in safe holding until you choose the design winner. This is terrific for people that are afraid to commit to a designer before seeing some examples. It is also a less expensive alternative than using a good freelancer or professional design firm.

- **Budget designers** – This is for the individual on an extremely tight budget. If you have virtually no money to start your business and you can spare $5, check out a site called Fiverr.com. The site is a great resource for getting small projects such as logo design, done on the cheap. Don't expect incredible quality, but certainly expect something better than doing it on your own, especially if you are not a graphic designer yourself.

- **Freelance designers** – Freelance is a very good avenue to go for logo design. If you haven't heard of Websites like Elance.com or Guru.com, be sure to check these out. On these sites, you can post your design project, and then have freelancers bid on them. You can review the freelancers' past project reviews and portfolios before selecting an individual to reward the project to. This is one of the best alternatives for high-quality design on a moderate budget.

- **Professional Design firms** – This is always an option. Personally, I would recommend going with a professional design firm hands down, each and every time. If you have the budget, do it, because this one single investment will probably pay back the most handsomely. People trust a brand with a very professional looking image. They just do. There are several professional logo

design firms on the Internet. Check out a
company called Logobee.com. But a simple search
on Google will reveal a long list of options for
professional logo design firms.

BRAND AWARENESS

If you're a small business or an entrepreneur setting out on his or her own, the startup incubation months are the most critical to your future success. Making people aware of your brand, and fostering a brand that breeds the following elements, are vital to a sustained and lasting business:

- Trust & Integrity

- Professionalism

- Unique Value

Everything that you do in business, or dealing with clientele, is a reflection of your brand. Make sure that you don't make careless mistakes like not following up when you promise to, or not delivering a project on time. Or, more importantly, not sticking to your proposed budget if you're a service oriented business.

People talk and your business can either spread like wild fire, or flounder like a sea bass out of water. The decision is entirely up to you, and how committed you are to your business.

In your day-to-day operations, take the time to analyze your unique value proposition and see whether or not you're fulfilling the value promises that you've made in there. This isn't just important in the Web 3.0 economy, however, it's more important in the Web 3.0 economy in order to set yourself apart, and differentiate yourself from the crowd.

In today's competitive marketplace, you have to do all that it takes in order to live up to the value that you propose to your clients. You can either create a very solid foundation for the future success of your company by creating brand awareness that breeds the three vital elements for success, or you can destroy any chance of success by not living up to your own hype.

3
DELIVERING YOUR MESSAGE

We all have a message in business, don't we? Some of us are pretty clear on that message, and some of us are a little bit murky. However, in order to succeed in the Web 3.0 economy, your message needs to be very clear, and very targeted. Whether you're starting out new, or you're already up and running, you can always refine or repurpose your message to target your specific customer profile.

Look, the Internet is getting crowded, very crowded, and there is a lot of noise out there. It seems like every time you logon to a social network you see someone else jumping up and down about his or her business. Sure, we don't always comment on it because it may be a friend or a relative, but you know the ones I'm talking about right? So, how is it that some people are able to deliver their message with tact, and others just seem to be tacky?

It's all about the method of delivery. Sometimes over-hyping yourself is not a good thing. You don't want to be the one actively promoting your own company, yet you do want to be actively promotion. What you want to do is breath positivity and life into your consumers to create raving fans that will do the promotion for you. How is this done? By providing an incredible amount of value.

By going above, and beyond the call of duty, you will be able to create a business that sets itself apart from the rest. Too many businesses are focused on doing the bare minimum of just what it takes to complete a job or a project for a customer, or better yet, deliver a product just on time. You have to go above and beyond the call of duty, and excel even when it isn't expected of you. This is the best method for the delivery of your message. This is the way to create raving fans.

THE VEHICLES FOR MESSAGE DELIVERY

In the Web 3.0 economy, you have to be well versed in the online marketing methods that will drive traffic to your site or your offer. It's plain and simple. Although the noise level has increased, the overall necessity to connect with the right consumers is still the same. It's just harder now than it was before.

There are several different channels that can deliver the marketing message to consumers on the Internet through the most cost-effective manners possible. Most of these channels will require a sincere and concerted effort on your part in the form of the investment of your time. Here are the areas that we will be covering:

1. **Search engine optimization** – Any Web 3.0 marketer or business, needs to understand the importance of search engine optimization, or SEO for short. SEO has changed and evolved, and it has been the topic of three of my past books, so it's safe to say that I know a fair bit about this subject. The number one most important online marketing strategy to marketing on a very tight budget is SEO. SEO will also affect nearly every other channel that you market through, so it has to always be in the back of your mind.

2. **Blogging** – Probably one of the most effective ways to driving traffic to your Website, blogging is an incredibly important channel that will be addressed. However, it's not just about writing any blogs. I will address what makes a blog post good, and just how to write that blog post so that it has the best chance of showing up in Google's search results.

3. **Social media marketing** – It's clear that social media is here to stay, but what's not clear to most people is how to leverage it properly to market a business or service. Social media can be a very powerful driver of business, but it can also hurt you as well if it's not utilized properly. I'll cover some of the best social media strategies available to new and existing businesses on the Web.

4. **Content marketing** – A largely untapped market primarily utilized only by professional marketers,

content marketing can become a strong driver of business for anyone. However, understanding how to leverage content marketing for your business type can be confusing at first. I'll uncover some of the strategies being used to propel businesses forward with the right kind of content marketing.

5. **Email marketing** – If you want to get a business off the ground and build a solid base of customers who trust you and stay loyal to your brand, you have to learn how to effectively communicate with them through email marketing. Whether you get their email addresses through permission-based sign-ups, free offers, or from past purchases, I will discuss the best ways to conduct your email marketing campaigns.

6. **Referral and review marketing** – This is a powerful driver of business. When tapped correctly, referral and review marketing can provide you with incredible amounts of new business leads. This involves leveraging the crowd the right way on Websites like Yelp and TripAdvisor.

7. **Public relations marketing** – We don't all have lofty budgets to venture out and hire PR firms. However, engaging in PR for your new business involves a few simple proven strategies that, when combined with some very powerful SEO methods and techniques, can provide a huge boost in

visibility for your new or existing business.

8. **<u>Video marketing</u>** – One of the most powerful methods of marketing on virtually no budget, video marketing on YouTube has become an incredibly large driver of traffic for most Websites new and old. However, understanding how to harness the power of YouTube is not all that simple, and most people simply don't know where to begin. I'll go over some simple strategies for driving traffic to any Webpage using a few methods and techniques on YouTube.

Sounds like a lot of ground to cover right? Well it is. But by being able to spread your message effectively through all these channels, you will open up the door to business success in the Web 3.0 economy. Now, not all of these channels need to be utilized by you, but they are all here and available for you when you're ready to leverage them.

What's important to understand is that, in the Web 3.0 economy, things have changed, because Google's search engine algorithm has changed. The way that Google indexes and makes a Website relevant has shifted and evolved, and it's important to understand the impact of how this affects you and your Website.

Understanding this new era of Google search will help you unlock some of the proven methods and techniques to driving traffic through any of the marketing channels with the highest efficiency and effect possible. Without some of this underlying SEO knowledge, you will have a much more difficult time addressing some of the marketing channels discussed in this book. SEO will impact nearly every single channel in some way, shape, or form.

4
UNDERSTANDING SEO

Search engine optimization, or SEO, has been the topic of three of my past books. In those books, I've covered a lot of ground on how to do SEO, but also what makes SEO different today. In the Web 3.0 economy, the name of the game is relevancy.

If Google doesn't think that you're relevant, then you're going to have an extremely difficult time getting found. If you can't get found, then your business won't grow. It's as simple as that.

So what's changed?

A lot has changed in the past couple of years. Google has dropped what some would consider being the atomic bombs of changes, ushering in a new era of SEO, and the art of being found on the Internet. These atomic bombs have altered the playing field, and have tightened the guidelines for being relevant, and being visible in search results.

SEO can be confusing and all consuming, because it encompasses so many different disciplines that all take time to develop and shape in order to boost a listing's visibility. There are so many different elements to address when you're conducting SEO work on a Website. These different elements both relate to work that's done on the Webpage itself, called On-Page SEO, and work done away from the Webpage, called Off-Page SEO.

While I won't be going into all of the specifics of SEO in this book, I will be using it as a reference point for how to do things in the Web 3.0 economy. So, it's important that you at least have a foundational understanding of how it works.

Anytime that you conduct marketing work on the channels of marketing referenced in this book, you have to implement some of this basic SEO understanding to help you in best formatting your content for high visibility on Google's search results.

Google Search SEO

Let's face it, the Internet has been fostered on the backbone of Google's search. I'm talking about online search through Google, because 83% of global search queries run through the search giant, according to *The Pew Research Center's Internet & American Life Project 2012 Tracking Survey*. That's an enormous figure, absolutely enormous.

So, it's important, in the new Web 3.0 economy, to understand Google's search and just what makes your Website or content on the Web relevant, and appear in search results. Because, let's face it, what better form of marketing is there than appearing in free organic search results listings? Not much. For this reason, it's important to understand Google's search, because most of the marketing techniques that I will be teaching involve guerilla-marketing tactics targeted from an SEO angle.

BEING CONSIDERED RELEVANT

Since the name of the game in the Web 3.0 economy is relevancy, your job, as a new or existing business, has to be to increase that relevancy factor as much as you possibly can. One of the underlying foundations to the relevancy factor is trust. If Google doesn't trust you, you simply won't have the foundation for relevancy. Trust breeds relevancy, and not the other way around.

Prior to February 2011 when Google dropped its first atomic bomb in the form of a massive overhaul to its search-engine algorithm, relevancy did breed trust. If you were able to follow a few very elite tactics in the SEO field, you could breed that trust with relevancy by tweaking and changing some components on your Webpage that would have automatically made you increase in relevancy on Google's search. Today, a lot of these tactics that were used, such as keyword stuffing, content cloaking, and others, are no longer considered acceptable.

In short, Google introduced several major changes that entirely obliterated the search-engine landscape and how search worked. It began rewarding unique content laden sites that offered rich user experiences, and demoting poorly written content sites that offered bad user experiences. During this time many of today's most popular blogs shot up to the top of rankings while those that were bending the rules saw themselves drop almost entirely, from not just the top of search results, but the indexes altogether.

Why is this important? Because, in the Web 3.0 economy, you need to make sure that you tackle your marketing from a trust perspective by breeding relevancy. Google needs to learn how to trust you, or you need to leverage sites that Google already trusts on the Web. Leveraging Google's trust for other Websites will be one of the main ways you'll spread the word about your product or service in the beginning, especially if you have a new domain name. This is also the way that you will increase Google's trust in your Website, by having other trusted Websites link to you.

Everything that you do, all that you post, foster, and breath into your content, has to be done with the final desired outcome of trust to breed relevancy, in the back of your mind. This boils down to creating content that adheres to some simple rules for SEO that will help it become more relevant, along with getting other sites that Google already trusts to link back to you.

Sound intimidating? It's not, don't worry, but it will require a good bit of effort on your part.

No matter what your budget, big or small, these are some of the highly-honed techniques being used by companies with large technical and marketing staffs that have this know-how. By arming yourself with this knowledge, you will be able to properly position your new or existing business in front of as many eyes as possible, virtually for free.

GETTING STARTED WITH SEO

The principles of SEO are basic, but you would be surprised just how few people either know them or follow them. To breed a foundation of relevancy through trust on your Website, you of course first have to have a Website in the first place. I'm going to assume that you do, or that you have one in the works, or are planning to set one up. Without a Website, you're really swimming the vast ocean of Cyberspace on your own with nowhere to call home. You need a Website, so that should be your first priority.

Aside from having a Website, there are other areas of content creation on the Internet where SEO will come into play. These techniques involve creating content on Websites that Google already trusts, also known as authority sites, which then link back to your own Website. Leveraging authority sites will be one of the main ways you will begin to drive traffic quickly to your own Website, and begin to build trust by having sites that Google already trusts, linking to you.

For this reason, it's important that you setup a Website. Furthermore, it should be a Website with an integrated blog, because unique content creation on your own Website will be at the very heart of your daily activities to create value and drive traffic.

The Trust Factor

A couple of important points about Websites first. When you're setting up a Website, you need to keep in mind that, if you're buying a new domain name, then your ability to get to the top of Google search results is going to become more difficult. Why? Simply put, Google just doesn't trust new domain names anymore.

Part of the trust factor that Google takes into the equation is just how new a domain name is. It's like walking into the bank for a business loan with a brand new company. The bank manager simply isn't going to trust you as much as if you had already been in business for a while. Even if you have a really good business that other people recommend, without some proven history of business operations, the trust simply won't be there.

The same notion applies to Google. If you show up with a new domain name, you just won't have Google's full trust. You'll have partial trust, but Google will keep a very close eye on you by not allowing you to get to the top of its search results right away. You will be placed in something called the Google Sandbox. However, if you have a domain name that Google knows about and has already indexed two or more years ago, then the trust will be there. At least trust through age that is.

There are three components of Google's trust that I

discuss in one of my books on SEO entitled *The SEO White Book – The Organic Guide to Google Search Engine Optimization.* Those three components are as follows:

1. **Trust through Age** – Trust through age is developed over time. There's no way around this. If you're a new entrepreneur with a new Website, this simply has to happen over time.

2. **Trust through Authority** – Trust through authority is developed by getting other Websites that Google already trusts to link to your own Website. When enough Websites begin linking to you that Google already trusts, you begin to earn your own authority, but this does not happen quickly.

3. **Trust through Content** – Trust through content is created and nurtured by continuously putting out excellent, well written, unique content, that provides value to people's lives. Content is king and to have content that rules the kingdom, you must provide a lot of value consistently.

SEO BASICS

To start building trust with Google you have to begin earning that trust by continuously putting out very well written content that is properly optimized, and also has a good amount of social factors, such as shares, likes, and tweets, along with other links from trusted Websites. This all sounds like a lot of work, and it can be.

What's important to always keep in the back of your mind is that in order to breed relevancy through trust, you must start with a foundation of very good content. When your content is good, the trust in your content is achieved, bringing you one step closer to relevancy in the eyes of Google.

On the Internet content is king, and if you have a good way with words, then you will be one step ahead of the game. You have to get used to writing content that is properly optimized for SEO that adheres to some basic SEO principles that involve keyword usage. Whether you are creating this content on your own Website by posting articles or Webpage content, or you are creating the content on an authority Website, you will always be targeting one primary keyword for that specific piece of content.

The keywords are going to be important here, because keywords are going to come into play along many of the different channels that you engage in some of these online marketing tactics on. Whether you are updating your LinkedIn profile, posting an article on an authority site, or adding video description to a YouTube video, keyword usage is going to be at the very heart of your guerilla marketing tactics to begin increasing your visibility, and driving traffic to your Website.

KEYWORDS

When we discuss keywords, we're really discussing something that is going to be at the heart of your online marketing strategy. No matter what you do on the Web to market your business, your focus always has to be on your keywords. Without knowing your primary keywords for your business, you won't have the basic foundational platform for effectively marketing online.

Your target then, for your business, is going to be a set of keywords that you want to have associated with your Website. Each article or Webpage that you post should have its own primary keyword that you will optimize that piece of content for. No matter what business you are in, there are some keywords that will help people find you. Some of those keywords will be much easier for you to climb Google's search ranks on than others.

For example, it will always be easier to rank better on keywords that are more specific as opposed to broad. This is where your customer profile and your unique value proposition come into play. The more you were able to hone down and pinpoint what value you will be providing to what specific customer, the easier of a time you will have allocating the right keywords.

In order to find the right keywords for your business, it's important to start with Google's own autosuggestion keywords. These are the keywords that automatically get suggested to you when you're typing in a search on one of Google's homepages. Whatever business you're in, and whatever value you're providing, you'll need to use those pieces of information during your keyword research phase.

Let's say for example that you are a graphic designer that designs flyers for realtors for their property listings. The first thing that you're going to want to know, is what people are searching for when it comes to graphic design services for the real estate market. This will require some brainstorming on your part.

In order to begin conducting your search, all you need to do is head to a Google search page online. When you go to Google to do a search keep a few things in mind:

As you type, the keywords that drop down as autosuggestions are the most common phrases typed resembling your input.

- The autosuggestions that drop down on Google's searches, apply locally for people in your area based on your IP address. This means that if you're located in Miami, Florida, you are going to see keyword autosuggestions for what people are typing in Miami along with global results. You won't see other local-specific keywords. For example, you may start typing "Graphic design," and see one of the drop-down items say, "Graphic designers in Miami," and if you're in Los Angeles, you may see "Graphic designers in Los Angeles."

• The keywords listed are not necessarily in the order of most searched to least searched so you will have to use another tool to determine how many people are actually searching for those terms. Google also provides this other tool, and it's called the Google Keyword Tool.

Let's say for example, that you want to find out what people are searching for on Google when you type "Real estate design services." When you do that you get the following few suggestions as autosuggestions:

• Real estate graphic design services

• Real estate interior design services

• Real estate web design services

• Design real estate services

The most applicable here would be "Real estate graphic

design services," rather than just "Real estate design services," because it is more specific. Remember, you want to get as specific as possible.

However, we don't want to just stop there, so let's try to expand on that. Now, when we type in "Real estate marketing," we get the following autosuggestions:

- Real estate marketing ideas

- Real estate marketing plan

- Real estate marketing tools

- Real estate marketing flyers

This would leave us with two very good keywords to go after, which would be the following:

- Real estate graphic design services

- Real estate marketing flyers

Those two keywords are also very good, because they are what you call long-tail keywords, which are keywords that are four or more words long. These types of keywords are much easier to target than shorter keywords such as just "Graphic design," or "Graphic design services," because they are more specific. And, because they are more specific, they will generally have a lower competition than the broader terms.

Remember, the more specific you can be on your keyword hunt, the easier this is going to be. If you have a new Website, and you try to go after a keyword like "Graphic design" on your own, you will fail. The term graphic design just by itself is a highly competitive keyword with a lot of search results. This will be impossible to get to the first page of Google with, especially for a new Website that is not yet trusted. For this reason, when you go after the long-tail keywords, you will have a much easier time getting ranked, and getting found.

Think about it, wouldn't you rather come up in the first few search results for a keyword that has very few searches done each month for it, or virtually not come up at all for a keyword with a lot of searches done for it? Of course, the answer would be to come up at least on the first page for a keyword with few searches.

According to a study done by Optify in December of 2010 (shown in the proceeding image), an average of 36.4% of people will click on the first ranking position on a Google search engine results page (SERP). What this study also shows is that 89% of searchers will not go past the first page of search results. That's a pretty staggering number, and while this study is a few years old, it still indicates the necessity for relevancy in search.

Rank #	Average CTR	Median CTR	Delta #n-1	Delta #n1
1	36.4%	25.0%		
2	12.5%	9.1%	-65.68%	-65.68%
3	9.5%	7.1%	-23.84%	-73.86%
4	7.9%	5.5%	-16.53%	-78.18%
5	6.1%	3.8%	-23.54%	-83.32%
6	4.1%	2.7%	32.01%	-88.66%
7	3.8%	2.6%	-8.26%	-89.59%
8	3.5%	2.0%	8.71%	-90.50%
9	3.0%	1.8%	-13.33%	-91.77%
10	2.2%	1.5%	-26.07%	-93.91%
11	2.6%	1.3%	17.80%	-92.83%
12	1.5%	0.7%	-42.37%	-95.87%
13	1.3%	0.7%	11.71%	-96.35%
14	1.1%	0.7%	13.72%	-96.85%
15	1.2%	0.5%	7.55%	-96.61%
16	1.2%	0.5%	0.10%	-96.61%
17	1.4%	0.5%	9.63%	-96.28%
18	1.3%	0.5%	-4.76%	-96.46%
19	1.4%	0.5%	9.57%	-96.12%
20	1.4%	0.6%	1.57%	-96.06%

Click Through Rates of Google US SERPs based on Optify data

If you can't show up in Google's SERPs, at least on the first page, then the likelihood of receiving traffic to your Website or article is going to plummet. For that reason, you are going to want to stick with a long-tail keyword for the simple fact that they will be easier to rank for. How can you know this for certain? You'll see how in the next step.

USING THE GOOGLE KEYWORD TOOL

Now that we have our long-tail keywords in place, we will want to do some research to find out just how many people are actually searching for these terms, and see just how competitive they are. Just as a point of reference, I will add the broader keyword, "Graphic design," to the list just for comparison, to make it a list of three keywords as follows:

- Real estate graphic design services

- Real estate marketing flyers

- Graphic design

Analyzing these keywords is relatively straightforward and does not require very much technical skill other than navigating to the Google Adwords Keyword Tool, which you can find by conducting a Google search for "~keyword." You can also simply navigate to: https://adwords.google.com/o/KeywordTool

Since Google provides this tool, it's an excellent way to look inside the mechanics of what terms are being searched for, and how many times they are being searched each month. The results from this simple tool will allow you to know, right away, how difficult it will be to rank for a certain keyword. And, although the tool is meant for advertisers, it can be used by anyone looking to understand and target their SEO activities.

As you can see in the image depicting the Google Keyword Tool, I added all three keywords into the search box, one on each line, then selected the "Keyword Ideas"

tab, and conducted the search. Now, you will need to login with your Google account into the Keyword Tool.

However, if you don't have a Google account, you can still use it, but you will be forced to enter in a CAPTCHA image confirmation code each time you conduct a search.

In the search results from the Google Keyword Tool, you will notice that there are three columns:

- **Competition** – this can be high, medium, low, or nominal (indicated with a hyphen).

- **Global Monthly Searches** – the number of searches conducted for this keyword around the world.

- **Local Monthly Searches** – the number of searches conducted for this keyword in your area (determined by your IP address).

In looking at the search results from the Google Keyword Tool, if you have a business that is very location based, then you should look at the local monthly searches, and not just the global monthly searches. However, for people that have a product or service that are not location based, the global monthly searches column should be used.

In looking at the results for the three keywords entered, you will notice that I have highlighted the "Real estate graphic design services" row to show you just how nominal the results back are. Now, if you are just starting out with a new Website, you are going to want to target a keyword like this as opposed to "Real estate marketing flyers," which has high competition.

In the list, you will notice that the "Graphic design services" also has high competition and being able to rank for a term like "Graphic design services," while good, is not really a laser-targeted term.

The more focused you are with your keywords the more likely you will be get people who are searching for that exact service clicking on your link. Just think to yourself, what you would type in when searching for your particular product or service, and go from there.

SELECTING YOUR PRIMARY KEYWORD

The purpose of this keyword research is to find yourself one primary keyword that you can then use for one Webpage or piece of content that you are going to optimize to drive traffic to your Webpage. Now, one important thing you have to keep in mind is that, you can go after the medium competition and even high competition keywords when you leverage some of the authority sites to build your content.

For example, when you begin doing content marketing, or video marketing, and you are using sites that Google already trusts, then it's okay to try to go after a keyword like "Graphic design services." That's because those trusted Websites will be much more likely to secure a top spot on a Google search than a Website that Google doesn't know anything about and doesn't trust.

You need to consider what channel you will be using your keyword in, and take it from there. If your Website is new, and you recently launched and you don't have a lot of authority, then do not try to go after highly competitive keywords on your own Website. This will make a lot more sense when you begin building content that you want to rank.

Your primary keyword is going to be important. It's going to be at the heart of your optimization efforts. Now, if this seems at all overwhelming to you, it really isn't, and your ability to grasp some of these concepts is going to make a considerable difference in your push to rise to the top in a crowded Web 3.0 economy. There is a lot of noise, but having some of these specialized skills to know what to look for and how to implement it, is going to set you apart from the crowd.

It really doesn't matter what you're selling. As long as you select a primary keyword that is very targeted and specific to what you offer, and begin to build content that is geared towards that keyword, you will see an incredible difference in the resultant traffic that will eventually come filtering in.

5
THE POWER OF A BLOGGING PLATFORM

Blogging has certainly become a buzzword. It seems like everywhere you turn, someone else is blogging. Why is that? Well, the blogging platform can be a powerful one, especially when leveraged properly. I'm not talking about blogging to make money on its own, that's actually rare. I'm talking about blogging to spread value for an existing product or service.

How does this work? Well, in the crowded Web 3.0 economy, if you're not spreading value, then you're going to fail. There are so many new businesses popping up everywhere you turn, that competition becomes more and more fierce each and every day. However, when you provide value to people in your specific industry, you become an authority.

R.L. ADAMS

Becoming an authority happens when you begin putting out and spreading so much value that Google takes notice. You create this value through blogging and providing useful information for your niche, no matter what it is, on a consistent basis. If you're a Web designer, then you talk about Web design tips. If you're a lawyer, you talk about legal tips. And the list goes on and on. No matter what industry you are in, you have to focus on providing value for that industry.

Once you begin spreading this value out there, Google will take notice. You begin getting links to your content, Google begins indexing you higher, and people begin sharing your information and blog links through social media channels. Your authority begins to accumulate little by little.

You may be thinking to yourself, well you don't want to spread out all the insider secrets to doing what you do, but that's a wrong frame of mind. You have to spread out as much value as possible. Literally, give people the farm. Tell them how things work, in detail. Analyze and deconstruct your industry, common practices, known pitfalls, and so on. As you do this consistently, you will build your Website's rank and increase its authority little by little.

People will begin to see you as an authority as your blog roll grows. When this happens, and you can successfully add calls to action to purchase whatever product or service you may be selling throughout your blog, you will see your sales begin to rise slowly and steadily. All this won't happen overnight. The blogging strategy is certainly a long term one, but one you should start immediately.

SPREADING VALUE THROUGH BLOGGING

No matter what industry you are in, you can spread value by blogging. But it's important to understand why this is so important, as opposed to just blindly going out there and doing it.

As you already know by reading the chapter on SEO, Google made some changes in the past to its algorithm. These changes have ushered in a new way of thinking by people, because it has changed the elements that Google is looking for when it comes to search.

You can no longer make your way up to the top of Google's search results without addressing some key factors. Without having a domain name that has some age, excellent content, and authority links, you will not be able to rank well. This has all created a vast fight for relevancy like never before. However, this time, marketers are forced to play by the rules.

This new era of search is the cornerstone of the Web 3.0 economy, the new Internet. Gone are the days of poorly-written content or badly-navigable Websites that rank high. Today, if you want to rank high you have to address all the factors that Google calls for and the best and easiest way to do this is by leveraging a blogging platform.

By blogging and creating unique content, you are building up your trust with Google. When Google finds your content, it adds it to its database, logging all of the specific details of that content, including when it was first published, the information in it, and what keywords it associates with it, just to name a few.

Being relevant in your niche is going to take some hard work on your behalf. As you begin to build content that is unique and provides value, Google will start to take notice. Furthermore, when this content is built not only from a value perspective for your particular niche, but also from an SEO perspective to optimize for your keyword, enormous progress for your site's ranking will begin to be made.

HOW TO BLOG FOR YOUR KEYWORDS

Blogging is one of the best ways to optimize content on your Website that will not only provide value, but will also rank well. This can also be considered to be article marketing, but not exactly in the traditional sense of that word. When you talk about article marketing, you're mainly referring to the network marketing industry known to put out a lot of low to medium-quality content in the hopes of having it rank high on Google.

When you blog for keywords, you have to create a blog that not only is very high-quality in terms of the value that it provides people, but also one that is laser-targeted to the primary keyword of that piece of content. In order to do this, you need to first come up with a topic that you know will help people in your particular niche. Usually, the best kinds of blog articles fall into the how-to category. This is what most people will be searching for.

In order to begin with your first blog, you should try to answer a common question in your niche. What is it that people usually want to know about or have problems with? Once you figure out what you want to write about within your specific niche, you have to pick an article title that will not only be attractive enough to be clicked on from an overall writing standpoint, but also one that has your primary keyword in it.

First let's take a look at what makes a great title for a blog. Here are the various different kinds of potential blog titles that you can come up with:

- **The Direct Title** – Most common amongst blogs is the direct title. The direct title is when you come up with the literal title for the article that you have written, nothing fancy, and nothing more. An example of a direct title would be *10 Lessons on Effective Online Marketing Strategies.*

- **The Indirect Title** – An indirect title for a blog article is a great way to peak the interest of potential readers. The ideal indirect title is indirect enough where it becomes interesting, but not too indirect that it becomes confusing. An example of an indirect title would: *The Perfect Storm of Effective Online Marketing Strategies.*

- **The How-To Title** – How-to titles are excellent ways to get readers clicking on your blog's articles. People on the Web generally are searching because they have a question about something, or they want to find something. An example of a how-to title would be: *How to Market any Business Online through Social Media.*

- **The Question Title** – The question title is a terrific way to peak interest. It has a somewhat indirect approach to a blog title depending exactly on how it's worded. An example would be: *Who Else Wants to Learn How to Market Online like a Ninja?* The assumption after reading this title is that, in the article, I will learn some very stealth like and effective ways to market online.

- **The Command Title** – The command title is telling readers what they will be able to do after reading your article. You are commanding, or informing them, that this will be the result of the information contained within your content. An example of this would be: *Skyrocket your Way to the Top of Google Search Results.*

- **The Reason Title** – This type of title is another popular one that is used by blogs today. The reason title offers readers a clue that they will discover the answer to something through reasons. For example: *101 Reasons Why you should Have a Blog*

- **The Testimonial Title** – A testimonial title can also be powerful when worded correctly. One example of a testimonial title would be: *Why Time Magazine Says He is the Greatest Leader to Ever Live.*

OPTIMIZING YOUR BLOG ARTICLES

Regardless of what type of blog title you select, you have to have your primary keyword for that specific page included in it. If you want to be able to rank, you have to follow some of the basic SEO rules for writing the articles, and it all focuses around your keywords.

Anytime you put a piece of content out there, whether you are writing the description for your business on your Facebook Page, doing a blog post, or issuing a press release, you have to make sure it is keyword centric.

In order to make sure that your blog is optimized for your primary keyword, you will have to follow a few basic rules of blogging for SEO that I will lay out here. The important thing that you want to keep in mind is that Google will analyze any piece of content to find out what it is about.

What most people make the mistake of doing is not

focusing on a single primary keyword. When you don't focus on a single primary keyword, you confuse Google into not understanding what your Webpage is about. Don't fall into this trap. Pick your primary keyword by doing the keyword research, and then focus your article on that keyword.

Here are the basic rules that your blog article must follow in order to optimize it for your keyword:

- **Select one primary keyword** – This rule also applies when you begin to market in other channels as well such as video marketing, content marketing, and press release marketing. You will always have to focus on one keyword for that piece of content. Make this a habit of knowing exactly what keyword you will be targeting your content for.

- **Write a long article** – A good rule of thumb when writing a blog article is to write it at a minimum of 500 words. However, extending it to past the 1000-word mark is a best practice when it comes to blogging. The content of your article should be optimized for your primary keyword by doing the following:

  o Place the primary keyword in the article title

  o Place the primary keyword in the article's description. If you use Wordpress to blog then you will not be able to do this unless you download an SEO plugin for your system. An excellent plugin is the Yoast SEO plugin that you can acquire for free and it will allow you to update the article's meta description field. That will be the field displayed on Google searches underneath the listing title.

o   Make sure that the article uses your primary keyword at a ratio of 2% to 5%. This means that for every 100 words you should have your primary keyword appear 2 to 5 times. Do not underdo it and do not overdo it to risk sounding spammy. You have to write your article so that it sounds good and doesn't sound like you've tried to stuff the keywords in.

o   Use your primary keyword once in the first paragraph of your article's content and also once in the last paragraph of your article's content. If you can use it in the first sentence and last sentence try to do that and if not just ensure it appears in the first and last paragraphs.

o   Uses the primary keyword in the H1 (Heading 1) tag – this tag can be selected by highlighting the text and picking the Heading 1 style from the drop-down menu in a system like Wordpress.

o Uses the primary keyword in the H2 (Heading 2) tag – this tag can be selected by highlighting the text and picking the Heading 2 style from the drop-down menu in a system like Wordpress.

o Uses the primary keyword in the H3 (Heading 3) tag – this tag can be selected by highlighting the text and picking the Heading 3 style from the drop-down menu in a system like Wordpress.

o Use your primary keyword once in bold font

o Use your primary keyword once in italic font

o Use your primary keyword once in underlined font

o Use your primary keyword once in the image ALT tag attribute. This can be defined in a system like Wordpress after the image has been uploaded and inserted into the post.

- Ensure that your Webpage URL includes your primary keyword in the name of the page – if you use Wordpress you can do this by turning on permalinks with the "postname" option.

- Any links to external pages must have the "nofollow" attribute, which tells search engines not to leave your page to go and index the page referenced by the link.

- Create at least one internal link from within the content of your article to another page or article on your domain.

- Create at least one external link to another Webpage on the Internet that uses your primary keyword with the "Nofollow" attribute.

This may sound like a lot of confusing information to digest, but it's important for you to understand the real mechanics behind how to optimize an article for your keyword. Because, today, in the Web 3.0 economy, it's not just about having good content, it's about having excellent content that is highly optimized for your keyword. Follow these rules listed above and you will be able to produce highly optimized blog articles for your keywords.

The proceeding image summarizes the key points that need to be addressed when blogging for SEO. You should keep this graphical representation handy and reference it when you set out to write a blog for your Website. These points apply to any content that you put out, however, on some authority sites that allow you to post blogs, such as Squidoo.com and others, you do not have the capability of modifying keywords in the same way.

Article Optimization

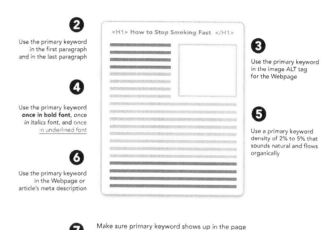

The hardest part about blogging with SEO in mind is not simply just optimizing the page. The hardest part is optimizing a blog for SEO that is well written without it sounding like you are trying to stuff the keywords into the article. You have to keep in mind that Google keeps track of everything. It has very intelligent algorithms that can determine just how well your article is written based on an analysis of the type of words used, and where they are positioned.

Don't try to fool the search engine by writing bad content. Not only will this be bad for your rankings on Google, but also by writing bad content, you will be adding absolutely no value to anyone's life. Without adding value, you will fail in the Web 3.0 economy. It's as simple as that. Take the time to write something that is unique, well researched, and well written, and it will pay off handsomely in the long run.

THE PURPOSE OF BLOGGING IN MARKETING

The purpose of blogging when it comes to marketing in the Web 3.0 economy is three-fold:

#1 – To Add Value

The first and foremost purpose to blogging is to add value to people's lives. When you add value, you attract more readers, and when you attract enough readers, people look to you as an authority on the subject.

Haven't you been browsing the Web for something in the past and found a blog or site that was so intriguing, that seemed to go above and beyond the call for information, and really provided an excellent, well-written piece of content that had you wanting to come back again and again? Maybe you then bookmarked this site and saved it for later in order to return? Sure, you have; we've all done this at one time or another.

Whether you're into tech gadgets or the latest travel info, we all have blogs and sites that we visit regularly, because we know that they are authorities on that topic.

#2 – For Organic Searches

The second purpose for blogging in the Web 3.0 economy is for organic searches, and to show up on Google's search results. This is not as important as adding value, but it is certainly a very important factor to blogging. When you create a well-written blog article that is highly optimized, you create trust with Google. When Google trusts your content, you are one-third of the way to a very highly optimized Webpage (the other two factors are age and authority through links).

However, the difficulty here is writing excellent blog articles that are optimized for Google searches. As soon as you can master this skill, you will find yourself that much closer to your goal of having a very visible site on Google's search engine.

#3 – As a Sales & Marketing Platform

The third purpose to blogging is to utilize it as a sales and marketing platform. When you blog and you provide value consistently, and you are able to earn the trust of your readers, then it becomes much easier to be able to sell from that platform.

Think about it for a moment. Wouldn't you be much more likely to purchase something from a Website that provided you with specific information on how something worked, or how to do something? For example, if you were looking for tips on how to write the perfect cover letter for your resume, and you found a very popular blog that detailed this for you, then saw a call to action to purchase resume-writing services for a very nominal fee, wouldn't you click on it? Of course, you would.

We are much more inclined to buy from Websites or places that we develop a sense of trust to. This is very easy to do with a blog, because by constantly creating value, then setting up that value to be visible on search engines, you immediately create trust over time. Why is that? Because users know that it is difficult to show up on Google's search results, especially at the top. If you're at the top of search results, or on the first page, then you gain instant credibility.

6
FIVE PRINCIPLES OF SOCIAL MEDIA MARKETING

One of the biggest changes to the Web over the past several years has been the emergence of social media. The outcropping of social media sites has hit frenzy levels, all riding on the backs of highly popular sites like Facebook, and Twitter. What this social media frenzy has brought to the Web 3.0 economy is a new level of collaboration and sharing that has taken the Internet by storm.

Since the rise of social media, we've seen Google enter into the fray with the launch of its own, now extremely popular social media platform, Google Plus. However, one other important thing has happened during all of this: Google has changed its algorithm to include social media shares from Facebook, Twitter, and Google Plus. This shift in recognition shows the importance that social media is now playing in our lives.

Although Google's algorithm is not all about the social media activity of a given piece of Web content, it is a very important aspect of it. Other factors include things like the number of backlinks, the age of the domain, and the value of the underlying content. However, social media links and shares are beginning to play a greater role in Google's search algorithm.

This is all very important, because it highlights just what you need to do as an entrepreneur in the Web 3.0 economy. By focusing on strategies for social media that work, you will be able to generate the largest possible amount of shares, likes, and tweets that you possibly can in order to boost that piece of content's visibility on Google's search results pages.

Professional marketers today use a number of different strategies and techniques to get their content shared and liked as much as possible. Some of these techniques include some very stealth like tools to do this, and some of the techniques simply involve the type of content that's distributed, and how you create a call to action.

What Works?

Ever logon to Facebook (or any other social media network for that matter) and seen someone over sharing again, and again? You know the one I'm talking about right? That one person amongst your group of friends, or someone you follow, who's constantly cheerleading their own work or causes. Yes, we've all come across these types of people in the past before, but it's important to take a look at sharing on social media to see just what works.

You need to take a look at this and analyze it as though

you were the person watching yourself share the information. You need to be on the outside looking in. How would you feel if you saw a link to the content that you just provided? Would you be inclined to click on it? Would it excite you enough to share it? Are you sharing too often?

When you ask yourself the right questions, and look at the underlying content that you're sharing, it's easy to see whether or not something is going to get traction in social media, or not. Your goal of course is to get that content shared as much as possible. But how do you do this? Well, first of all, you have to have a solid base of people in your immediate inner circle to start with. If you have 1,000 friends, people in your circle, or followers, it will be much easier getting traction on your social media shares than if you only had say 100 of the same.

However, aside from having a large base of fans, followers, or friends, for social media sharing to really work, you have to ensure that you are adhering to five principles of interaction. No matter what you are sharing, whether it's a photo, a video, a blog article, literally anything, the purpose of your interaction on social media is to attract, engage, connect, convert, then retain.

You want to be able to create raving super fans that will help to tout your products and services to their own friends. But this doesn't happen overnight. Creating a social media strategy requires consistent and concerted daily effort on your part. You have to put in the time to make sure that you're interacting with people to create, nurture, and grow your circle of followers, friends, and fans.

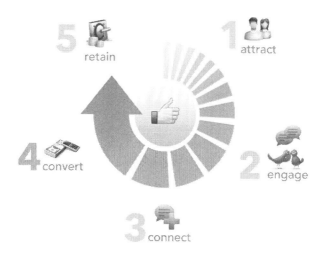

#1 - ATTRACT

In order to draw people into your shared media content, you have to be able to attract them. This attraction can happen in many different ways, but you have to understand some basic principles of marketing through attraction for this to work.

The art of attracting people through social media means that their eyes have to pass the scan test. As people scan through their social media feeds, they are quickly going from one status or tweet to another, seeing which one catches their eyes. They are scanning.

When people scan, they are scanning titles for something that pops out at them. If you recall the section on blogging where I discussed writing effective blog titles, here is where you get to leverage that work that you did in writing an attractive title that included your primary keyword.

If you have a title that can attract someone enough to pass the eye scan test, then you know that you've done a good job with your title. You have to think about what you yourself would click on. Go back and review the types of titles, and make sure that you come up with something that is attractive enough to get clicks.

#2 - ENGAGE

Once you've attracted someone to your post, you need to be able to engage them for long enough to hold their attention. Remember, no one wants to just read some plain old boring article about different services that you provide. That will not engage or entertain whatsoever.

The best way that you're going to be engaging to your friends or followers on social media is to share your content through the power of storytelling. If you are a good storyteller, then you will find this very easy, and if you are not, well, this will be much more difficult. But, this is certainly a skill you can develop with practice.

Simply put, people just don't want to hear about your business. They would rather hear a story, and if that story happens to relate to your business, then you will hold their very fleeting attention span that much longer.

Why do you think people are so infatuated with

television and the movies? It's because people love to be entertained and engaged. They want an escape from the drudgery of work and business for the most part. If you're not engaging and entertaining you will quickly lose people's interest, and no one will want to read your article, let alone share it.

Tell a Story

People love stories. For that reason, when you share on a platform like Facebook, Twitter, or Google Plus, make sure that you tell a story. Aside from having a blog or post title that will attract, you need to engage in order to keep them there. Whether you are sharing a photo, a video, or a link to an article on your blog, back it up with a story, and make sure that your content is in line with the story.

For example, I have a close friend, Erica, who is a professional resume writer for corporate executives, and she told me this story about how she wanted to advertise her services through Facebook, but didn't want to come off so "salesy." She lamented to me that she hated seeing people fervently pitching their businesses around the clock, and she didn't want to be "that person," as she put it.

I told my friend that she should tell a story, so I dug a little deeper and started asking her some questions about her work, and whether or not she could think of any interesting stories that came to mind. She told me she did have one recent interesting story about a lady named Rosie that came to her after 10 years of working for the same company, with the desire to get her resume polished to hunt for a new job.

Rosie had an incredibly low morale at her, then present

employer, because her department was merged with another department. And her new department head was someone who she had a past history of not getting along with.

Erica went on to tell me the story about how Rosie's manager had done just about everything to undermine her over the past 10 years of working at the company. Finally, this manager had begun to purposefully park in Rosie's parking spot, which was a considerably shorter walk to the office than her own. This was the final straw for Rosie, apparently.

Once Erica had finished telling me the story, I told her that she could easily take Rosie's dilemma, and potentially change her name if she had to, then spin it into a blog post as a story about her resume writing services. Within this blog post, she would of course have to ensure that she optimized it for her keywords, but also that she effectively told Rosie's story in a manner that would engage and entertain.

Once I had finished explaining all of this to Erica, she immediately became excited by the possibility of that story, and how she could turn it into an excellent article that also provided some resume writing tips as well. I of course told her that was an excellent idea and just smiled.

I did however add one piece of information to Erica's arsenal for the story, and informed her that once she finished telling the story, she needed a call to action. This call to action would help to achieve the second to last principle for social media marketing: convert.

#3 - CONNECT

Connecting with your audience is one of the key principles in social media marketing. Once you've been able to attract and engage them, you have to be able to connect, because that connection is the true meaning of social networking. Anytime you're able to deeply connect and affect people through your engaging stories, you will captivate your audience enough to have them become loyal fans and followers.

What some people forget at times, that are trying to use social networking solely for profit, is that connection is at the root level of its interaction. If you are unable to establish a connection, you will lose your audience. What does this mean? Well, connecting can be done in very many ways, but really, it means to bring out the human side in you.

People like to interact and connect with other real people. Even if you're running a business, you have to bring the real you out and into the open. Allow people to see the more human side of you by talking about your family, placing pictures of your kids playing sports, or a million other things that can be done to show people a glimpse into the real you.

If you're telling good stories, this connection can happen fluidly within the story itself. It's your goal to always create that connection, because that connection is the very fiber of the strings that will keep that fan intact.

#4 - CONVERT

At the end of telling Rosie's story, I told Erica she needed a call to action. I told her she could use the call to action as a way to help encourage people to share the story, make someone like her page, or tweet it, or as a call to visit her services page where people could purchase one of her professional resume writing packages.

Having a call to action is imperative in any type of marketing material that you put out. Some people forget, or completely leave out the call to action, because they think that it is obvious that if a customer is on a sales page with a buy now button, that they don't need to tell the customer to buy now. You do need to tell the customer to buy now.

The call to action is a signal to the brain. It may be a conscious signal, but often times it is an unconscious signal. By having a sentence that tells them to buy now, you are extending the literal call to action by telling them what to do next. You will be surprised at just how well this will work.

Other ways of placing calls to action would be to use similar terms for an urge to buy. For example, instead of coming out and saying, "Buy now," you could have a sentence that says, "By now you should realize how much you need a book like this." Can you see the "By now" is a subconscious feed to the mind that triggers purchase mentality without actually saying it. This works exceptionally well.

#5 - RETAIN

Once you have people as fans, followers, and customers, you have to be able to retain them. So many people get caught up in making the sale that they forget to implement practices that would help retain their existing base of fans.

Today, in the overcrowding Web 3.0 economy, people don't want to be part of something that isn't active or interesting. If people have joined you by either following you, or becoming a fan of your business, keep them interested. Implement the three E's of retention:

1. Educate

2. Entertain

3. Empower

This requires consistent work on your behalf, so make sure that you set aside time in your schedule to dedicate to your social media activities. Try to limit yourself to an hour or two each day and don't allow yourself to get too sucked in or carried away. If you have a problem overindulging in social networking, find a way to cut yourself off at a certain time. Set an alarm for yourself if you have to.

R.L. ADAMS

BUILDING A FAN BASE

When I talk about building a fan base, I'm of course referring to platforms like Facebook, and Google Plus, which allow you to setup a page for your business, then invite people to join that page by liking it, or adding it to their circles.

To most people, when they think about building a fan base, they immediately think about inviting every single friend that they have to like the page simply because they are friends. I would highly discourage you from doing this. When you try to actively promote your business to friends in this manner, people get annoyed. You have to put yourself in their shoes. How do you feel when you get an invite from your friend to like a page? Usually, you probably ignore it unless it is somehow relevant to the conversation.

Relevancy – that's the name of the game isn't it? In the Web 3.0 economy, companies are vying to be relevant.

Since Google has now changed the rules, people are clamoring at every possible tidbit of information that they can devour in order to try to stay one step ahead of the curve. However, what most people end up doing is simply over self-promoting themselves and their businesses, in turn detracting more people than they attract.

In order to attract people you need to make sure that you setup a system for that attraction. You have to have an excellent piece of content loaded and ready to fire. Even better, if you have an automatic gun filled with dozens of rounds of excellent content just waiting on the ready to be fired, you can actively promote and gain traction to your business page without people turning a sour face. Why is that?

People simply enjoy good content that is presented in an engaging manner. If you can tell a story through the content, or relate the content to a story that provides a real sense of who you are, people will keep coming back for more.

What you want to try to do when you're interacting with people on Facebook is to not only create a fan base, but to create *super fan*. What's a super fan? A super fan is not only someone who has given you their basic details as a fan, but they have also purchased from you and got another fan to purchase from you as well. They are your biggest cheerleaders.

So how do you go about getting potential fans to become super fans? Well, it all has to do with your ability to adhere to the principle of engaging. If you are very good at engaging, then you will create super fans, but it won't happen overnight. Super fans are nurtured and created over an extended period of time of sharing. If you want to create super fans, here are some of the basic strategies that you need to adhere to when you are engaging on social networks like Facebook:

#1 – The Human Element

People like to interact with other real people on social networks, and if they find that you like to come out from behind your business, and show your true self through shares about your personal life, you will create much deeper and lasting connections. You can create the human element in your engagements by taking 1 in every 5 posts that you post, and making it a personal post.

For example, maybe your son just scored a goal at his school's soccer game and you decide to share that, or maybe, your daughter just got her first straight-A report card, and you decide to share that. Maybe even, if you're having a bad day share that. As long as whatever you share can be shared with tact, and can engage, and bring out the human element of the man or woman behind the scenes, you will create a deeper, and more lasting connection.

#2 – Become an Authority

No matter what your niche is, becoming an authority will set you apart from the rest of the Web 3.0 crowd. There are so many fan pages and business pages out there that post nonsense, that in order to set yourself apart, you need to post about topics of interest in your industry.

If you have to, setup a Google News Alert so that you hear about trending topics first, then share these with your fans and followers. After a while, people will begin to recognize that you are a true authority in the industry, and that they hear the important news about what's going on in your niche first, from you.

#3 – Encourage Fan Dialog

After you post on Facebook, or any other social network for that matter, stick around for a little while to create a dialog with your fans or followers. Just think about a real-life situation: if you were speaking to a friend, would you say something then walk away? Probably not, unless you were in a fight, but on Facebook, stick around, and encourage a two-way dialog with your followers.

The more you encourage dialog with your fans, the more you will keep them interested, and interacting. This is key to nurturing fans into super fans. You want to create a good level of interaction that doesn't have them forgetting that you even exist, but also doesn't have you overdoing it. Create a back and forth, and allow the dialog to come naturally, don't try to force it.

When you create dialog and make a post active on Facebook, it encourages fans to share that post. If that post happens to have a link to your Website for an article that you wrote, then this will be counted in Google's algorithm for search visibility. This is considered an authority link since Google trusts Facebook's Website, and any links or shares coming from it have a high factor towards your visibility.

If you post interesting and engaging posts, then you are encouraging shares, which will eventually lead to more visibly on Google. Can you see how the simple act of telling an engaging story with a link to your Website can benefit you in more ways than one in the Web 3.0 economy?

#4 – Spreading the Word

There's no better promotion than word-of-mouth promotion. In order to get fans talking about your company and spreading the word, you have to create giveaways. By creating giveaways, you begin to invite interest and interaction through a much higher level than your standard interaction.

You can setup a system to reward your fans or followers who invite their friends to your content or giveaway, through apps on Facebook such as the Wildfire app - http://www.wildfireapp.com. By setting a system for reward, you will further encourage your existing fan base to spread the word for you.

#5 – Track and Analyze

Of course, no true marketer's work is complete until they are able to successfully measure the fruits of their labor. Get in the habit of tracking and analyzing your activities on social networks. Facebook provides an array of tools to do this with. However, there are other third party tools as well.

You can use a Website like Topsy – http://www.topsy.com - to gain instant social insight or you can check out any of the other following Websites as well:

http://www.socialbakers.com

http://www.socialmention.com

http://klout.com

WEB 3.0 STARTUPS

http://www.twitterfall.com

http://www.hootsuite.com

http://friendorfollow.com

http://blekko.com

7
GOING VIRAL

We've all heard of the term *Viral Marketing*, before and it applies to the notion that ideas can spread like viruses. The term, viral marketing itself is attributed to Harvard Business School graduate Tim Draper along with Harvard Business School faculty member Jeffrey Rayport. Rayport popularized the term in an article written for *Fast Company* entitled, "The Virus of Marketing."

When most of us think about something "Going viral," we think of videos, namely, videos on YouTube. There are many viral videos that come to mind when you think of the video platform but its social media that now allows these ideas, or pieces of content, to spread like viruses, much quicker than ever before.

Anytime that you're approaching content creation you want totackle it in a manner that would be consistent with the potential for going viral. While you may not be a professional marketer, there are a few effective viral marketing strategies that you yourself can implement to set yourself up for the greatest success possible. While you can't guarantee that something will go viral, you can do your best to set yourself up for it.

Viral marketing doesn't have to be just videos. It can be anything. Think about the other types of content that spreads like viruses. Viral marketing applies to virtually any type of content on the Web. It can be a news piece, an article, a video, a photo, a Facebook post, a Tweet, and everything else in between. But, for something to go viral, it has to be both interesting and fascinating at the same time. It has to captivate its audience in some way or another. Not just anything will go viral. You know that.

Still, some of us try with all of our marketing might to take things viral. So, what exactly does it take for something to go viral? Here are some tips on a few things that will help you along the route to taking something viral. Although these are not going to guarantee that a video goes viral, it will help you mold and shape your video to give it the potential to do so.

1. **Create your content** – Whether it's a photo, a video, a short story, or anything else in between, create your content, but conceive it first. Do some research into what has worked in the past. You've seen all the viral content that spreads around on Facebook like wildfire, so take a deeper look into it. Ask yourself some questions about what made it so viral, then try to replicate your content on the same principles.

2. **Get the attention of someone big** – This is when viral content hits a crescendo. When the content gets to someone big like a celebrity who then shares it, and a major article or news piece is published referring to it, the viral bug explodes, moving out in every single direction at light speed. Of course, you can't guarantee that you will get the attention of someone big, but you can give your content a good start. Begin by posting it to places like:

   a. Reddit.com

   b. Digg.com

   c. Stumbleupon.co

   d. Tumblr.com

   e. Facebook.com

   f. Twitter.com

   g. Plus.google.com

3. **Be controversial** – People like controversial videos. They tend to go viral. But, there's a fine line between being controversial, and going overboard. It's only you that can determine where that line is going to be based on the type of content that you're creating.

4. **Be shocking** – Sometimes you just need to shock people. This is a popular kind of viral photo or

video, and usually involves some shocking situation, or person doing something shocking. The problem with being shocking is that it has to be authentic. If it's not authentic, it most likely won't get the traction that you're hoping for.

5. **Be funny** – Of course, it's not just about being funny, but funny photos and videos certainly make their rounds on the Internet. Some of the most popular ones have been released by cast members of Saturday Night Live, but making a funny video or creating a funny photo with a quote, is easier said than done.

6. **Be relevant** – Think in terms of current events, and the application of your piece of content to what's going on in the news right now. Try to piece together an indirect relationship of your photo or video, and what's happening with current events. Maybe you use a quote to do this on a photo, or maybe it simply happens in the content of a video as a parody of a serious situation.

7. **Be brief** – You have to be able to produce your content with brevity. You won't hold people's attention spans for more than a few minutes if you want something to go viral. Try to conjure up the best way that you can possibly deliver your message in the shortest time possible.

8. **Call to Action** – If you're creating viral content for a business then you have to have a call to action. No matter how big or small that call to action is, you have to have one. If your content starts spreading without a call to action, then you really haven't done your job right. What kind of call to action? Well, that's for you to decide.

You can't guarantee that you'll be able to take something viral, but you can do your best to provide the best content possible in the shortest period of time. There have been several excellent examples of viral videos and photos, and they keep occurring all the time. Do some research into viral videos by doing a Google search for "Best viral videos" to see what has worked in the past.

8
EFFECTIVE CONTENT MARKETING

In the Web 3.0 economy, you have to set yourself apart from the crowd. You have to provide value, a lot of value. Of course, this is a resounding theme, but this is where the fusion of SEO, and all your other activities come into play. If you've had some practice already with writing in your blog and creating very well written and unique articles from an SEO point of view, then this will add fuel to that fire.

Content marketing is part of what's called attraction marketing. I attract you by spreading value in the form of my knowledge. Look, people out on the Internet are always searching for ways to do something. They have a thirst for knowledge and information like never before, and you have to be the one that will provide that value in your niche. Content marketing extends beyond just blogging on your own blog; it steps out to the authority sites on the Web.

How does it work? Content marketing works in a very basic and straightforward manner. You provide excellent content that you then give away for free to people searching for that content. This is where SEO comes into play, because when you post content on Websites that Google already trusts, and are highly optimized for your primary keyword, you will skyrocket to the top of Google's search results. If your content is good, you will see an enormous amount of interest in what you've written, and you'll be able to produce leads and sales from this if you're setup with the right calls to action for your products and services on your blog.

The best types of content marketing are the research, or how-to kinds of content marketing. For example, let's say that you're in the Web design industry. What you could do, is create a piece of content that talks about the top 10 mistakes that Web designers make, and how to avoid them. Within your content, however, you would need to link to content on your site that is inline with the same keyword as the content that you are creating.

Your first step, before you go creating content on another Website, is to make content on your own blog that you will link the external content to. Why is that? This is for SEO purposes. In this evolved Google search world, you have to build relevant content that links back to more relevant content. This is going to build authority. Remember the mention I made about having authority links? Well, the best kinds of authority links are those that come from other unique content on authority sites.

Here's an overview of what the process would look like:

1. Write your well-researched, unique blog article centered around one specific primary keyword, on your Website.

2. Create a unique piece of content marketing with the same primary keyword in mind, on the authority site.

3. Create a link from the content marketing piece on the authority site, to your blog using the same primary keyword.

Content Marketing

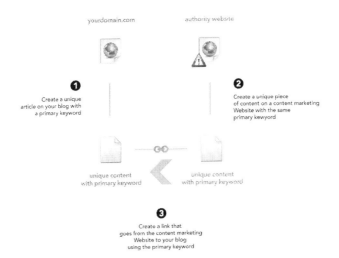

When you create a link from a very popular Website that has authority, such like the ones that you will be developing your content marketing on, you provide yourself with a very important boost in Google's visibility.

Why is that? Google already trusts these Websites. These Websites have a lot of age, authority and unique content so that when you create content on their sites it will instantly be rankable in a very high position on Google's search results.

This is an excellent way to boost the visibility for any startup. You don't need a budget to do this, and you can do this on your own. Furthermore, each piece of content that you create and rank will help your with your overall Google rankings by creating trust through content and authority both at the same time.

As you create more pieces of content that rank well and link to your own unique content on your blog, you will boost the overall ranking of your blog over time.

So, how do you get started?

Creating really good content for marketing online is a bit of an art form, and requires some time and research on your part. To extend on the example posed before, let's just say that you're in the Web design market, and you wrote a blog about the top 10 mistakes that Web designers make, and how to avoid them.

First off, on a blog like that, you would have a primary keyword such as "Top website design mistakes," or "Top web design mistakes." Your article that you write would have to be optimized for that keyword. Afterwards, when you create your content marketing piece, you create another article, or unique piece of content with the same keyword focus. Finally, you would link the two together with the link coming from the authority site to your own site. The link itself would be the primary keyword.

When you set out to create your content, it's important to understand the types of content marketing that can be conjured up:

- Articles and blogs

- Word documents

- PowerPoint presentations

- Infographics

- Instructional and how-to videos

Here are some tips for starting your content piece out:

1. **Pick a topic** - To get started with content marketing, you first have to pick your topic. Your topic would be in your respective niche of course, and it would be a topic that would help to educate and provide value to someone. Your topic can be a negative topic such as "Mistakes", a positive one such as "Resources", or one that discusses industry trends such as "Traits."

2. **Pick a number** – When you pick a number, you're deciding to yourself just how long your piece is going to be. Popular numbers are 3, 5, 7

and 10, but your content piece can be any length. The number is going to signify the amount of things or ways that you will be explaining how to do something. For example, "Top 10 most common website design mistakes," or "Top 5 productivity tips for working from home," and so on.

3.   **Pick a modifier** – When you pick a modifier, you're differentiating your how-to topic's tips to come before or after something. For example, you can say "Top 10 Mistakes to Avoid <u>before</u> you Launch a New Website," but you can also change it to say "Top 10 Mistakes to Avoid <u>after</u> you Launch a New Website." Simply changing the modifier of the phrase can change the entire article.

WHERE TO POST YOUR CONTENT

There are a few authority Websites that make it worthwhile to post your content to in terms of receiving good visibility on Google. These Websites have very high PageRank – a measure of traffic volume – that allows content posted to soar to the top of Google's search engine results pages when it is optimized properly.

Here are the Websites that you can use to post authority content to on the Web, that you would then optimize and link back to your own content:

- **Squidoo.com** – These are blog articles, but you are limited to placing links only in the suggested links area and you cannot post links throughout the article itself. Still, if you develop a good piece of content in the form of an article, this is an excellent place to post it. However, you have to be careful not to violate their Terms of Service (ToS) by posting spammy content, or content that is specifically intended as advertisements. If you do this, then the content will be removed or not approved for posting in the first place. Make sure that the content you post is interesting and informative, and not a direct advertisement.

- **Tumblr.com** – Tumblr.com is a high PageRank Website that allows you to post just about anything and have it rank well if it's optimized properly. You can post links, text, quotes, audio, and video here. A lot of professional marketers leverage Tumblr.com for their content marketing work. It provides a simple and easy to use interface for posting and sharing content.

- **Slideshare.com** – This Website, recently acquired by LinkedIn, has a very high PageRank that can be used to literally take content marketing viral. This is because so many people visit and share on this site, that marketers now flock to it to post content. The content that you post can only be in the form Word documents or PowerPoint presentations. You also have to be careful not to violate their Terms of Service (ToS) as well; otherwise, you will see your content be removed. Do not post spam or content that is advertising in any way. Simply post content that will engage, educate, and provide value to readers with a link back with your primary keyword to the corresponding article on your site.

- **HubPages.com** – This is an easy to use high PageRank Website that offers a very simple user interface. The site allows you to post content freely and offers fewer restrictions than some of the other content marketing Websites discussed here. HubPages.com is also a high PageRank Website, and if you optimize the content properly with a link back to your site, this will give you a huge boost in terms of SEO value in the eyes of Google.

- **Scribd.com** – This Website is another site that is similar to HubPages.com, and also with a very high PageRank. On Scribd.com, you can post articles, PDF files, Word documents, PowerPoint presentations, and so on. Any file that you post will be indexed by Google, so if you are posting PowerPoint presentations, be sure to use text that will get indexed, as opposed to overloading it with images. The best program to use is Microsoft Word, where you can indicate heading tags and other HTML elements within the document, that will get translated when Google crawls the content.

- **YouTube.com** – There's not enough that can be said about YouTube. Google loves YouTube videos, especially ones that provide value. When you shoot a YouTube video, make it informative, and engaging. Try not to be dull and boring so that you can get people to like your video and share it with others. Embed your video into your articles or Webpages that target the same content or keyword. In addition, provide some transcription information into the description of the YouTube video, which works really well for SEO purposes. YouTube videos get ranked very high so if you want to target a keyword search, shoot a YouTube video and optimize it.

Engaging in content marketing can be a lot of work. However, it can also be some of the most rewarding work that you put in to the marketing efforts of your new Web 3.0 business. Sometimes, this can get overwhelming, so create a schedule for yourself, and focus on creating a few very good pieces of content each week.

Make sure that the content provides value, is interesting, and informative. Then, do what you can to spread that content across all of your social media channels as well. This will create a solid foundation for the content to get found and devoured by the content hungry market of consumers looking for answers to the questions you've solved in your content pieces.

9
EMAIL MARKETING

Email marketing is an extremely powerful tool for spreading your message and getting sales. But, just like the overall theme in everything else in the Web 3.0 economy, your email marketing has to provide value. The Web has pushed back against spam and useless emails, and they are no longer plaguing inboxes like they once did. While email marketing can be a very powerful tool, it will only work if you truly harness the power of your unique value proposition.

What is it that you're selling? What niche are you in? Is there a set of tips you can send out possibly on a weekly basis if you really thought about it? This is where your blogging and your industry expertise come into play here. Since you will already be writing unique, well-written, and well-researched blogs, along with content marketing inline with those, it's very simple to transition this work into email marketing.

First off, you have to come up with a reason why people are going to want to subscribe to your email list. You have to provide something of value upfront in exchange for their email address. As a startup company in the Web 3.0 economy, you have to do some initial legwork in the beginning to get yourself setup. You have to provide something for them in exchange.

So, what are you supposed to provide? Well, most people will default to the free ebook offer. The free ebook offer provides visitors to your site with a free ebook containing some type of valuable information in exchange for their email address. You should really go out of your way to create an excellent eBook, and don't just throw something together.

Try to target something in the range of 5,000 to 10,000 words with excellent content and value. You can use your free ebook as an upsell for your products or services, and set it up so that your free ebook is emailed automatically upon a person subscribing to your email list. This is simple to do by utilizing an email list system from any of the following three companies:

- Aweber.com

- Getresponse.com

- Constantcontact.com

When you setup your email system, make sure that you engage the autoresponder. Place the ebook into an autoresponder email that will get sent out immediately after a person signs up. Whether you setup a landing page, or a download page for the ebook, it's important that they have access to the ebook instantly after joining your email list, or they may get a little agitated.

EMAIL MARKETING TIPS

Although email marketing can be a powerful driver of business, it's easy to get carried away. Nobody likes receiving numerous emails in a row from anyone, especially a company that they still don't really know a lot about. You have to approach your email marketing with tact, and setup a schedule that will have emails go out on a periodic basis, at roughly once or twice per week.

These email marketing tips will be vital to your success in executing and conducting an effective email campaign for your startup or existing business:

- **Make subscription easy** – Place the signup above the fold on your Website (above where the page first gets cut off by the scroll bar). If you have a blog, place it in the right-hand or left-hand column. Make sure you add verbiage about a free ebook download. You can generate sign-up forms through any of the three major email list systems I mentioned.

- **Tell the readers what to expect** – Readers are going to want to know what to expect in your emails. Aside from telling them about the free ebook that they get just for signing up, make some sort of mention of what types of emails they can expect to receive from you. Whatever niche you're in, this verbiage should be geared towards helpful tips for that industry.

- **Send an instant welcome email** – An instant email is a necessity in email marketing. As soon as someone signs up to your email list, ensure that they are sent an email by utilizing the autoresponder of whatever system you decide to use for email marketing. Provide a short welcome message, and describe to them what they can expect from you in the way of content.

- **Only email periodically** – It's easy to get carried away, and some online marketers will tell you to email every day, but you will literally lose all of the worthwhile people on your list if you do this. Keep your emails down to once or twice per week and make them count. Craft very informative emails that provide an excessive amount of value.

- **Craft killer subject lines** – Don't make the email subject lines sound boring. If you do, your click through rate will be horrendous. Take the time to craft killer subject lines and don't just send anything out. Be careful not to use deceptive tactics like "RE:" or "FW:" to indicate the email is a reply or a forward. You will lose trust very quickly like this.

- **Deliver insatiable value** – Always provide value. Always. Make sure you never send out an email that's less than the best you can absolutely do. Provide real value in your emails and you will see incredible results. If you can't set yourself apart from the crowd then you'll see your efforts flounder.

- **Know the spam rules** – Make sure you read up on the CAN-SPAM Act at the following URL - http://www.business.ftc.gov/documents/bus61-can-spam-act-compliance-guide-business. Not following some of these rules can not only see you lose subscribers, it can get you into legal hot water.

- **Write copy that sells** – This comes back to your ability to engage your readers. In order to write copy that sells, you have to be you and tell a story that shows your human side. Relate to your readers in a way that only you can, and deliver the information with passion. It's very easy to tell when a person sending us an email is passionate about what he or she is writing.

- **<u>Talk to them like a friend</u>** – Talk to your subscriber like he or she is your friend. Give it a personal feel. Don't come across too stuffy or impersonal. Make that connection, and make it seem more like you're having a dialog. Even consider using "P.S." and "P.P.S." at the end of the email to make it seem even friendlier.

- **<u>Make it easy to unsubscribe</u>** – Not only is this a *should* but it's a *must*. By way of the CAN-SPAM Act you must have an unsubscribe link in your email somewhere (in addition to a physical address). If you use an email system from the likes of the three that I've recommended, it will be included for you automatically.

- **<u>Place a call to action</u>** – It's important that you place a call to action in all of your emails. Whether you want them to visit a link or purchase a product make sure to only include one call to action, but do it three separate times. Place it once towards the beginning, once in the middle, and once at the very end. The call to action is a necessity if you are going to have effective email marketing campaigns.

- **<u>Track and analyze stats</u>** – No marketer would be doing their job if they were not tracking and analyzing the statistics of their efforts. In email marketing, you can track and analyze statistics such as clicks, and email open rates through the major email systems themselves. Companies like Aweber.com, Getresponse.com, and Constantcontact.com provide you with the tools to view statistics on their Websites for the campaigns that you send out. This is also an excellent way to test different campaigns with different subject lines to see which ones work the best.

10
HARVESTING RAVE REVIEWS

The new Web 3.0 economy has ushered in a level of honesty unparalleled before. Businesses are forced to provide excellent service, lest risk the wrath of customers posting negative online reviews. Online reviews can either make or break a business so it's important that you do what you can, no matter what business you're in, to harvest rave reviews for your business.

Websites like Yelp have exploded in popularity. Yelp, a popular online business directory and review Website, sees approximately 40 million visitors per month and has over 20 million customer reviews for businesses that it has listed. Yelp keeps companies honest because it doesn't allow a company to change or amend a review once it's posted, only respond to it. As long as the review is a real and honest review, then Yelp will not remove it, no matter what.

What does this mean for you?

Companies must leverage Websites like Yelp and TripAdvisor in order to harvest reviews because customers rely on this knowledge in order to pick service providers in just about any industry. However, we all know how difficult it is to generate reviews for a new business, so how do you get started?

No matter what you do in the end, your true business ethic is going to come to light. Some people do what they can to purchase business reviews in the beginning to give themselves a good head start, or they ask family and friends. However, I think that this is a very poor strategy. Why?

People today aren't stupid. They know that companies go out there and purchase reviews, and they've gotten smarter at analyzing the reviewer to see what other past reviews they've posted. However, people continue to do it, and some swear by it, but it's something you should not engage in. What happens is that, if you engage in a practice like this, and then your service or products does not live up to the hype, you are going to get some scathing reviews that will all but eliminate anything positive said about you.

Still, it is said that a single negative review can do more to depress a business's sales than a single glowing review. So how do you go about getting customers to rave about you in reviews on sites like Yelp? Here are some tips:

- **Always provide excellent service** – This goes without saying, but still, it needs to be said. You must always provide excellent service above and beyond the call of duty, if you want to generate rave reviews by customers for your company. This is true no matter whether you are a new business or an existing business. In the Web 3.0 economy, you must stand out by providing impeccable service to your customers.

- **<u>Always suggest that customers leave a review</u>** – Whether you are listed on Yelp, TripAdvisor, Elance, Guru, or any other site that hosts reviews that customers can browse, you should always suggest that a customer leave a review. This should be done in the beginning of your interaction as a way of keeping you honest, and also informing the customer of your commitment to provide absolutely excellent service.

- **<u>Place a link in your email signature</u>** – One of the best ways you can always be encouraging people to leave reviews about your company is to place a link in your email signature. This is a more subtle way to approach customers for reviews. If you already have some positive reviews, place a small badge in your email signature that highlights your commitment to excellent service.

- **<u>Promote on social media</u>** – Social media is an excellent resource for marketing your business page on sites like Yelp and TripAdvisor. Use the opportunity to spread the word, but make sure that you do it through an interesting and engaging story. Don't just throw a link up there that no one will click. Make it count.

- **Place a badge on your Website** – Sites like Yelp and TripAdivsor, along with others in the service industry, allow you to place badges on your Website that will encourage people to go and see your reviews posted online. By placing a badge on your site, it shows your commitment to excellent service, and will invite other customers who will place reviews after they purchase from you.

- **Respond to all reviews** – When you respond to reviews, you display your commitment to potential customers that you care what people think about your business and services. Don't allow a review, good or bad, without a thorough response from you as the business owner. Customers who search for businesses on Yelp will appreciate your commitment and attention to detail by responding to all reviews.

- **Promote on Yelp** – Yelp allows businesses to promote their services on its Website. If you promote on Yelp you will most likely find customers interested in purchasing your services that will leave you reviews. If you have a small budget, then you may want to consider running a small promotion to generate new business, and the potential for reviews.

11
CREATING A PR STORM

The public relations industry is built upon relationships. When you have the relationships with media writers and reporters, you can easily pitch your ideas to them or your clients' ideas. When you don't have the relationships, it makes things a bit more difficult, but not impossible.

People pay thousands of dollars per month just to have a good PR company on board helping them to promote their business. Because by paying that money, they are purchasing an instant set of relationships, developed and nurtured over years and years. However, we all know that most startups and existing businesses simply don't have the budget for a firm to handle their PR, and can't wait years to develop relationships with the media.

To remedy this situation, some take to handling their own PR work, and some simply choose to ignore PR entirely. However, as a startup or existing business, you have to ensure that you address public relations. Even if you start out small, you can ramp up to create a PR storm, as long as you do the work and follow through a little bit each day.

If you can be considered relevant and an expert in your industry, then you'll not only have your stories featured, but you yourself may be brought on during segments, or for interviews. This is excellent exposure for anyone, especially a startup company looking to spread their message. If you, as the founder, can be featured on national, or even local news, then you add that much more credibility to your business.

ALLOCATING TIME FOR PR

The problem is, where do you find the time to juggle handling all of these marketing efforts, all at once? Simply put, it's all about the scheduling. Now that you've had a good primer on creating marketing content to promote your products and services online, it's a relatively easy transition into promoting yourself to the media. However, there are some things that you'll need to do first.

Anytime you're approaching the media, you have to set yourself up as an expert, or an authority. They have to trust that you're an expert in your field, and they have to see you as relevant. See how there's a resounding theme here now to where Google has gone with its search algorithms? For the longest time, Google didn't use many of the important trust factors that it uses today to determine relevancy.

BECOMING RELEVANT TO THE MEDIA

Today, just like Google requires now, the media needs to trust you. So, what do you do to earn that trust from the media? Well, the first off you need to let them know that you exist. You can do this by gathering the media contact information for reporters and writers in your niche. You can do some simple searches online, and gather their email addresses, names, names of publications, and phone numbers if you can find them.

Once you're armed with information for the media in your niche, you have to pitch them a story, and pitch yourself as an expert in your niche. If you have specific credentials that make you an expert in your niche, outline those. But, if you don't, simply explain why you are good at what you do, or why you are knowledgeable and trustable.

Put together a one-page biography on yourself and your business and then formulate the story you are going to pitch to them. If you've already done a fair bit of blogging and content creation by this point, then you'll have a base to work with, but you should always take a look at the best angle to approach your story from the industry that you're in. What works in your niche? Here are some pointers:

1. **Humanize the story** – People always want to see the human factor of a story. Just like in social media, the better you are in relating your business or idea into a story that brings a human element into play, the more traction you are going to get. This will take some practice if you're not already a seasoned writer.

2. **David v. Goliath** – People love to read about the underdogs prevailing. It's the source of many plots for movies and books. Try to see if you can approach your pitch from a David versus Goliath point of view.

3. **Use Surveys** – Using surveys to support your point is an excellent way to craft a persuasive news story. However, only you can determine which types of surveys to use to support the points you're trying to get across. Find surveys and make sure to cite your sources.

4. **Leverage Trending Topics** – The better you are at leveraging trending topics in the news media, the better your chances will be to get your pitch picked up by a writer or reporter. Find ways that you can adapt your story to trending topics in the media. Even if you get a small sound bite, it's one that you can credit to yourself to add to your resume of being an expert in your niche.

Selecting a story angle is important when it comes to PR. While you may run into some brick walls trying to promote yourself, just like with all your other marketing activities, you'll eventually find what works, and what doesn't. The important thing to realize is that this type of marketing takes consistent follow up and approach. Some PR professionals spend weeks and months pitching the same story with different angles before it gets traction.

You have to think about your business from several different points of view. What about your business makes it different and special? What about your story humanizes it? Come up with something that delivers your business in a story format, with passion. This will come across to anyone that reads your pitch.

PRESS RELEASES

Issuing press releases is a great way to create your own PR storm. While the direct approach to reporters and writers will work some of the time in getting you discovered and noticed through mainstream media, it won't work all of the time, especially if you lack the tenacity to constantly follow up. For this reason, turning to online press releases can be a haven in an otherwise cluttered world of relationships and press networking.

The approach to press releases can be broader than your approach to a specific media professional. When you target a media professional in a specific industry such as entertainment, or business, it's important to take a look at the type and style of stories that they write, and attempt to adapt yours to their usual approach. When you issue an online press release, it should still be a story that has a human angle, but it can be a broader story about your business.

The terrific thing about issuing online press releases is the immediate exposure and coverage. First off, Google already trusts some of the major online press release Websites like PRWeb.com, so if you purchase the additional exposure through them, then your press release will see huge visibility on Google. Second, reporters already comb through media releases on a daily basis looking for stories that peak their interest. But, this is where your talent of writing a very crafty killer title to your story will have to come into play.

If a reporter likes what they see about your story, then they will contact you or whomever you've listed as your media contact, for an interview for their own piece. This is incredible exposure for just about anyone, and depending on the media outlet that the individual is from, this can result in national and even international press for your business.

However, getting a reporter's attention is difficult today. Your story has to be very good and very relevant. If you followed along with some of the points on writing the story, and you've crafted an excellent piece, then you should have no difficulty gaining some traction. Still, if you can't write well try to outsource the writing for your release on a site like Elance.com or Guru.com, because this single piece of content will be incredibly important for you.

When you put together your press release, follow the same rules that I've suggested for article optimization. You have to write your press release from an SEO angle that is geared towards your primary keyword. Make sure that keyword appears according to the same set of rules that I've described in article optimization, and makes sure that your press release falls in the range of 500 to 1000 words. Try not to get too carried away with the number of words on a press release, because you will lose people's interest fast if your writing isn't perfect.

When you're ready to send out your press release, check out some of the following Websites that allow you to issue online press releases:

- Prweb.com

- PRnewswire.com

- I-newswire.com

- Pressdoc.com

12
POINT, CLICK, AND SHOOT

It's clear that Web 3.0 economy has created a dramatic shift in relevancy as a result of Google's new search rules. But, what isn't clear to most people is how to leverage those rules to the best of their ability. As I discussed earlier, Google places heavy weight on a domain's age and authority. If a domain name has been around for a long time, has a lot of other trusted Websites linking to it, and has great content, then it becomes very relevant.

YouTube is one such site that is very relevant. Now, it could be because YouTube is owned by Google, but the Website itself has become its own popular search engine, and seasoned marketers are leveraging YouTube for all its worth. Because YouTube is such as trusted site on the Web, any content posted to it that is optimized for certain keywords, will rank extremely high.

If you do some searches on Google, you will notice on most of them, you'll find YouTube videos that come up in the top few results. Why should you care? Because, just like in content marketing when you're posting articles and presentations, videos posted on YouTube can be an enormous boost for your Website's traffic.

When you are preparing yourself to point, click and shoot your first video, make it inline with a topic that you've already come up with and written a blog about. If you're camera shy, you don't necessarily have to appear before the camera, you can simply have a screen shot of a notepad or PowerPoint presentation as you change the slides and speak in the background.

In the Web 3.0 economy, you need every single advantage that you can get as a startup, or as an existing business. Shooting and publishing YouTube videos is one such advantage. It not only aids with ease of content delivery, it also provides for an incredible boost for your Website's visibility when the video is optimized properly and linked to the corresponding blog on your Webpage.

Not only does the YouTube video provide great SEO value with a powerful backlink from a very trusted Website, it also humanizes you. Although you don't need to appear in front of the camera, the actual video itself, even if it features just your voice, brings forward the real you. When people can hear your voice and you sound authentic in trying to provide value, people will realize it, and they will flock to you. Do this on a regular basis, and you will watch your YouTube channel explode with subscribers.

When you're ready to begin shooting your video, here is an outline of some of the points that you should follow when creating that video:

1. **Conceive** – You first have to come up with the concept for the video. If you're doing a video strictly for SEO and visibility on Google your direction will be different than if you're doing a video for the purposes of entertainment in the hopes of going viral.

   a. **Target audience** – Take a look at your customer profile. Is this who the video is for? Keep in mind who you're targeting and tailor your video, language, and any visuals to that target audience.

   b. **Topic** – Selecting the right topics to shoot a video about could be as simple as wanting to create a video to boost the visibility of a blog post that you created. The nature and content of the video you create should be reflective of the topic you select. Try to stay within your niche.

   c. **Message** - Ensure that the message you convey in your video is clear, concise and to the point. Don't wander off on tangents or you will lose people's interest. Make it count and make it impactful and informative. Add value in some way, shape or form to the viewer, whether through information or entertainment.

2. **Capture** – Once you have your concept together, simply capture your video, and edit with any major software application that you can find to get the job done.

   a. **Keyword rich title** – When you upload the video to YouTube, make sure that you create a keyword rich title. Follow the title writing recommendations in the blogging chapter, but also try to start your title with your keyword.

   b. **Keyword tags** – YouTube allows you to add keyword tags to your videos. Go through all the major ones that you've researched that would apply and add them here.

   c. **Summary** – The summary will be the field visible in Google searches underneath the video title. This is also considered meta description, so make sure that your keyword appears in the first sentence of that description, then follow along with the article optimization rules as best as you can within the confines of YouTube.

   d. **Playlist** – When uploading a video to YouTube, you can select other third party videos that can be offered in the playlist. Select videos that are close in comparison

to yours and try to find popular ones. This
playlist is used in YouTube's algorithm for
search when recommending videos to
people who search on YouTube so choose
wisely.

e. **Closed captioning** – On YouTube, you
   can upload a closed captioning file to go
   along with your video. You can take
   advantage of this by using a keyword rich
   file that provides relevant information on
   your video. This information is indexed in
   Google's search.

3. **Promote** – This is where your newly found social
   media skills come into play. Learning to promote
   your video means spreading it out into the world
   through as many channels as possible.

   a. **Social Media** – Leverage every social
      media channel that you can to spread links
      to your video.

   b. **Embed in your Blog** – Make sure to
      embed the video into the corresponding
      blog article on your Website. Also, be sure
      to add a link from the YouTube video to
      your blog for a high PageRank backlink to
      your site.

13
THE ROAD TO STARTUP SUCCESS

No matter what type of economy you start your new business in, the road to startup success is long. There are so many challenges along the way that it's easy at times to throw your hands up in the air and give up in silent resignation. But, just like with anything else in life, good things come to those who work hard.

The Web 3.0 economy is a crowded one, but it is also a much more relevant one. By changing its search algorithms, Google has sent a very powerful message to the Web: be relevant. These changes are at the heart of what makes marketing in the Web 3.0 economy tick today.

Google's integration of divergent online mediums into its search engine results has sent another powerful signal in the marketplace: be socially relevant. Google knows the power of crowds, and it is beginning to rely on crowd sourcing information more and more in its search results. The likes, shares, and tweets by various Internet users can help to solidify a listing on Google's search rankings, or see it fall if it lacks social credibility.

So where does this all leave you?

Well, you know that to start a business in any economy, you have to take on a lean approach. You have to be mindful of what you spend and how you spend it. However, it's also important to be mindful to the factors that will affect your visibility in the new Web 3.0 economy. By understanding the factors that play a major role today in how ranking and visibility works, you can effectively leverage methods and techniques that virtually cost nothing to help you create relevancy.

When you are relevant, you are visible. But to become relevant, you have to be able to build trust by successfully tackling multiple different online marketing disciplines all at once. However, if you move forward with the resounding theme of always providing value in both your business and the content that you put out online, you will create a solid foundation for the success of virtually any business.

It's easy to get discouraged, but always be mindful to set your goals, then modify your approach as you go along until you hone in on what works for your specific business.

Always keep pushing. Always keep striving. Put your best efforts forward into marketing your startup and eventually good things will start coming your way.

OTHER BOOKS BY THIS AUTHOR

If you enjoyed this book on startup marketing, I would really appreciate it if you could take a few moments and share your thoughts by posting a review on Amazon. You can do so at the following link - http://www.amazon.com/dp/B00BYZB68U

I put a lot of care into the books that I write and I hope that this care and sincerity come across in my writing because in the end I write to bring value to other people's lives. I hope that this book has brought some value to your life. I truly do.

Also, feel free to also take a look at some of the other books that I have available on Amazon. The following titles can also be found that I have authored:

- *SEO White Book – The Organic Guide to Google Search Engine Optimization* - *http://www.amazon.com/dp/B00BUOPFHI*

- *SEO Simplified – Learn Search Engine Optimization Strategies and Principles for Beginners - http://www.amazon.com/dp/B00BN7PGEY*

- *The SEO Black Book – A Guide to the Industry's Secrets - http://www.amazon.com/dp/B00B7GIVSE*

- *How Not to Give Up – A Motivational & Inspirational Guide to Goal Setting and Achieving your Dreams - http://www.amazon.com/dp/B00BSB02KI*

- *Kindle Self Publishing Gold – Unlocking the Secrets of How to Make Money Online with Kindle eBooks - http://www.amazon.com/dp/B00BQJB5QM*

- *Kindle Marketing Ninja Guide – Killer Marketing Strategies for Kindle Book Marketing Success - http://www.amazon.com/dp/B00BLR40FC*

I wish you all the best in your Online Marketing pursuits.

All the Best,

R.L. Adams